Class, Bureaucracy, and Schools

Class,
Bureaucracy,
and Schools

The Illusion of Educational
Change in America

MICHAEL B. KATZ

FOREWORD BY STEPHAN THERNSTROM

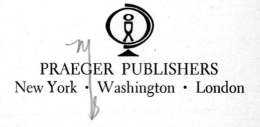

PRAEGER PUBLISHERS
New York · Washington · London

PRAEGER PUBLISHERS
111 Fourth Avenue, New York, N.Y. 10003, U.S.A.
5, Cromwell Place, London SW7 2JL, England

Published in the United States of America in 1971
by Praeger Publishers, Inc.

© 1971 by Praeger Publishers, Inc.

Library of Congress Catalog Card Number: 76–143975

Printed in the United States of America

For Rebecca and Paul

Contents

Foreword

By Stephan Thernstrom

We hardly need yet another book to tell us that something is drastically wrong with the American educational system. But we badly need new insight into *how* that system came to be what it is. Without that, without a clear understanding of the historical roots of the contemporary educational crisis, real change is impossible. The dominant characteristics of our schools today are the product of a long history, and those who hope to alter those characteristics need to know their origins and enduring functions in order to act effectively.

This probing and unsettling little volume is an essential starting point. Michael Katz is a brilliant young historian whose first book, *The Irony of Early School Reform: Educational Innovation in Mid-Nineteenth Century Massachusetts* (1968), was widely hailed by scholars in the field as a pioneering study. The crusade for educational reform led by Horace Mann, Katz revealed, was not the simple, unambiguous good it had long been taken to be; the central aim of the movement was to establish more efficient mechanisms of social control, and its chief legacy was the principle that "education was something the better part of the community did to the others to make them orderly, moral, and tractable."

Although it focused on the middle third of the nineteenth century, Katz's volume was rich in implications for the present, implications of interest to ordinary citizens as well as to scholars. But these, for the most part, were left implicit. Now, happily, Katz has taken on the more ambitious task of speaking directly to the nonspecialist about the connections between the past, the present, and the future of American education. He has assessed the fateful decisions that were made in the late nineteenth century, the time when the essential shape, purpose, and function of the modern American educational structure were fixed; he has identified the ways in which these structural features continue to operate in schools throughout the society; he has clarified the difficult choices that confront the educational reformer today. And he has done all this in lively, crisp, pungent prose.

Katz is radically critical of American education and of American society as a whole. He presents here, with caustic wit, devastating evidence of the failure of perhaps the most vaunted of our national institutions to operate in a manner consistent with the mythology that surrounds it. The schools, he argues, do not liberate the individual and open up opportunities for social mobility to the disadvantaged. The social-class biases that pervade the educational system and the bureaucratic control structures that give force to those biases produce schools that "reflect and confirm the social structure" by processing children to fit into "slots roughly congruent with the status of their parents."

He does not, however, fall into the easy romanticism of too many contemporary radicals, whose indictments of what is are rarely accompanied by any thoughtful consideration of what might be. One of the finest things in this book is its sophisticated and tough-minded appraisal of the very real difficulties involved in reconciling such conflicting and desirable goals as racial integration, community control, and pedagogical innovation. Katz's modest "concluding suggestions for reformers" will disappoint those who refuse to face up to these conflicts, but I find them immensely suggestive.

The historian who whores after Relevance is likely to produce history that is neither good nor relevant. Hasty incursions into the past in search of evidence to buttress a political position typically yield results of little value to either scholar or citizen. But, when a first-rate historian who has mastered the complex evolution of an important institution offers his seasoned and disciplined reflections about where we have been, where we are, where we should go, and how to get there, a book of unique value can be the result. This is such a book.

Preface

I shall begin this book with an excerpt from the most damning indictment of American education that I have yet encountered. It is the report of a task force on the exclusion of children from the Boston public schools, *The Way We Go to School* (Boston: Beacon Press, 1970). The report's power derives partly from the horrors it describes and, as well, from the traditional values it exemplifies. For, on the basis of this report, the Boston public school system stands condemned not only by romantics and radicals but also by the most long-standing and fundamental of American ideals.

Chapter VIII of the report describes the characteristics, attitudes, and role of attendance officers. This discussion provides a fitting introduction for what I have written in this book:

> Between September, 1968, and May, 1969, over 700 children were taken to court primarily due to their being truant from school. The attendance officer is instrumental in this court action: he acts as the prosecutor, gathering evidence against the child and presenting it in court. It is at the discretion of the officer whether to take a child to court.

When one member of the Task Force asked the Co-Head how he feels about taking children to court, he responded: ". . . we are often dissatisfied with the disposition because if a child gets off, others learn that going to court is not such a big thing. They don't fit the crime with the punishment anymore. That's the whole problem. . . ." Asked what kind of crime he was referring to, the Co-Head replied: "The crime of truancy."

Because of their dissatisfaction with court proceedings, the officers often use other methods in providing their services: "You've got to cajole or threaten. It becomes a question of forcing those wards [sic] to school. We tell the parents we'll take them to court or we'll stop their [pay] checks. It's not legal, of course, but we tell them that anyway."

The predisposition of the attendance officers to rely on court action and threats of court action stems, in part, from their backgrounds and training. The position of attendance officer is a civil-service one, with preference given to disabled veterans, veterans, and other people in that order. Aside from their military backgrounds, most of the officers have training in police work. Most of the forty-six officers now in the Department are former policemen.

In the course of our investigation we were told by a number of people, some within the School Department, that the position of attendance officer is a "political plum"—a highly paid, permanent position meted out on the basis of friendships and political connections. The salary, for example, is fixed at $15,400 per year, one of the highest paid positions within the School Department. (It is more than a teacher with a Ph.D. degree can make at the highest salary increment.) The annual Attendance Department budget for salary alone is . . . $741,000.

Recruitment procedures for the position are as questionable as are the officers' qualifications. The examination for the position is given sporadically. . . . A professional who works in a community agency reported to us that he has been attempting to take the examination since 1968. He has received no answer to his letters requesting the date of the next examination. When he goes in person to take the exam he is told that it was just given, or that there are no openings. Yet, he reports that new officers have been added to the Department several times during the period.

One School Department official told us that when there is a vacancy the position is filled immediately by a friend of an attendance officer or high-ranking school official, before interested citizens can compete for the opening. In support of this, he points out that none of the officers are black, Puerto Rican or Chinese, and that only four are women. . . . One of the Co-Heads . . . characterized all truant children as being "less intelligent, less well-scrubbed, crude, careless, and with pungent speech." Upon rebuttal of his statement, he responded: "Let's face it, these people are not school prone; they're just not. Their morals are certainly indicative of this."*

We often think of attitudes like these as characteristic of the nineteenth century. In fact, they are. One purpose of this book is to show the persistence of educational attitudes and structures in American cities over the past century and a quarter. Another is to proclaim and to account for the illusion of educational change in America.

* Pp. 57–60.

Introduction

On a street corner in a Brooklyn slum there stands a modern school, a massive concrete block in the middle of an asphalt playground. Like an ancient fortress, it has long, narrow slits in place of windows. If I were a kid that building would frighten me. So would the windowless school that stands in Harlem. They remind me of the old schools in working-class neighborhoods of London, surrounded by high walls. Those walls testify that the first compulsory schools were alien institutions set in hostile territory. The same point could be made about contemporary educational fortresses in New York; one international feature of educational history that has remained intact is the separation of the school from the working-class community. Sometimes the outward appearance of a school has relevance to the activities that take place within it; that was so in those first compulsory schools in late-nineteenth-century England. It has often been so in New York; even the occasional capture of schools by progressives cannot change the assumptions that underlie their architectural design.

Consequently, there is logic in the choice of schools as objects of capture by communities seeking political and social emancipation. For the schools are fortresses in function as well as form, protected outposts of the city's educational establishment and the prosperous citizens who sustain it. In their own way, they are imperial institutions designed to civilize the natives; they exist to do something to poor children, especially, now, children who are black or brown. Their main purpose is to make these children orderly, industrious, law-abiding, and respectful of authority. Their literature and their spokesmen proclaim the schools to be symbols of opportunity, but their slitted or windowless walls say clearly what their history would reveal as well: They were designed to reflect and confirm the social structure that erected them.

There is a great gap between the pronouncement that education serves the people and the reality of what schools do to and for the children of the poor. Despite the existence of free, universal, and compulsory schooling, most poor children become poor adults. Schools are not great democratic engines for identifying talent and matching it with opportunity. The children of the affluent by and large take the best marks and the best jobs.

That fact cannot be explained either by genetics or by theories of cultural deprivation; it is the historical result of the combination of purpose and structure that has characterized American education for roughly the last hundred years. The purpose has been, basically, the inculcation of attitudes that reflect dominant social and industrial values; the structure has been bureaucracy. The result has been school systems that treat children as units to be processed into particular shapes and dropped into slots roughly congruent with the status of their parents. There is a functional relationship between the way in which schools are organized and what they are supposed to do. That relationship was there a century ago, and it exists today. This is why the issues of social class and bureaucracy are central to understanding the public school.

Purely contemporary analysis obscures this point. To appreciate the interweaving of structure and purpose in education it is necessary to study its origin and development. Today's educational structures are historical products; they represent patterns that have become deeply embedded in American society and are enormously resistant to change. The techniques with which the system maintains its equilibrium have themselves become traditions. We have become so accustomed to these ways of responding and to the assumptions enmeshed in existing structures that it is difficult to isolate and examine them clearly. But we gain detachment by looking at their origins. We can in fact pick out the moments when familiar features were new and controversial. We can analyze the interaction of social goals and social forces that entrenched those features in social history and ensured their survival over alternate proposals.

That is what this book attempts to do. Chapter 1 is schematic; it sets out to show the major organizational alternatives proposed for urban public education at a time when its structure was problematical. It makes the connection between social-class purposes, bureaucratic form, and the origins of urban school systems. By contrast, Chapter 2 is very concrete. Its purpose is to complement the essentially static analysis of organizational models with illustrations of educational development and an examination of the confrontation between bureaucracy and social reform.

This book concentrates on the years between 1800 and 1885; that was the critical period. My thesis is that by about 1880 American education had acquired its fundamental structural characteristics, and that they have not altered since. The final chapter considers that claim and the failure of subsequent reform movements which it implies. It considers the present moment in educational reform as well and concludes with a few concrete suggestions for reformers.

It may help the reader to understand the structure and details of this book if he knows something of its argument in advance. The central proposition that the book advances is, as I have said, that the basic structure of American education had been fixed by about 1880 and that it has not altered fundamentally since that time. The various parts are designed to demonstrate that point. They show how and why that structure came to be and, at less length, point out the continuities throughout the past century. If the central proposition is accepted, five important questions follow, and the book is designed to answer these, both implicitly and explicitly. First, did anyone propose alternatives to the structure that emerged? Second, was the establishment of that structure, regardless of alternative proposals, somehow "inevitable"? Third, what have been the interconnections between the major dimensions of that structure, or between its shape, its purpose, and its function? Fourth, why has the structure remained so resistant to reformist thrusts? And fifth, what is the moral of the structure's history for contemporary reform, or, must structural change precede "educational" change?

Acceptance of the proposition that the basic structure of American education has remained unchanged rests, quite obviously, on the definition of "basic." I mean by the term that certain characteristics of American education today were also characteristic nearly a century ago: it is, and was, universal, tax-supported, free, compulsory, bureaucratic, racist, and class-biased. Those features marked some educational systems by 1880; they diffused throughout the rest of the country in a sequence that roughly paralleled urban growth. In the first two chapters it will be apparent how education acquired these characteristics. In the last chapter I shall point out what is almost self-evident: that they persist today. I do not deny, or wish to imply that I deny, the introduction of important innovations—for instance, the kindergarten, vocational education, guidance, testing, and various new curricula, to name but a few. These have all made a difference, but they have not touched or altered the structural features I have outlined. It is to me, to use a very crude metaphor, as if the characteristics noted above form the walls of a box within which other sorts of change have taken place. The box is filled with objects that can be moved around and rearranged, but the walls themselves remain solid. Moreover, if I may extend the image for a moment, only objects that can fit within the box can be put there. Thus there is a congruence between the purposes and functioning of innovations that have entered the schools and the structural basis of the educational system itself.

This brief elaboration of my proposition should give meaning to the questions posed above. To take the first: Did anyone propose alternatives to the structure that emerged? Historians too often have conceived of educational history in simple moralistic terms: Good men—reformers of vision, dedication, and courage—proposed in embryo form the school system we now have. Opposing them were selfish, narrow-minded bigots interested in saving money and keeping the working classes down. We now know that this is nonsense, because we can see the consequences of those early proposals and because we find it hard today to accept simple, one-sided explanations of human behavior. But we must also reject the traditional story because of its constriction of historical vision. We must not accept the notion that there was but one educational proposal around which controversy revolved. On the contrary, in the first half of the nineteenth century four different proposals, four alternative modes of organizing public education, competed for acceptance. Each of them rested on a distinct and identifiable set of social values, and the competition among them reflected and expressed wider value conflicts within society, just as the Ocean Hill–Brownsville case or discussions of community control and decentralization do today. They were, additionally, real alternatives; examples of each did in fact exist. In Chapter 1 I shall present these models at length and the values on which they rested.

The second question is largely one of causation. The model that emerged victorious was the one I call incipient bureaucracy, and the question is, Why? Did bureaucracy triumph because it was somehow "inevitable"? It is a question of some importance for social theory as well as for historical inquiry. Perhaps naively, I see one implication to be that bureaucracy *is* inevitable. Given a complex, technological society and a complicated and massive social task like universal schooling, there is no other way of proceeding. Bureaucracy is neither good nor bad in this point of view; it is a social fact, a necessity. If we want schools, hospitals, welfare, or manufactured goods, we must have it, for the alternative is chaos and anarchy. If the logic of that point of view is accepted, then reform directed against the notion and existence of bureaucracy is at best romantic and, in any case, useless. It is better to accept the reality and permanency of bureaucracy and to improve its operation.

But if bureaucracy in education is inevitable, it did not seem so to some men who lived at the time of its creation. This is one moral of the story of alternative propositions. Some men at different points in time, in the nineteenth century and today, have been able to conceive of ways other than bureaucracy for managing the affairs of modern society. It is thus difficult to accept the proposition that bureaucracy is the only means through which social tasks can be accomplished.

In fact, on closer inspection, it appears that bureaucracy is inevitable only when men confront certain problems with particular social values and priorities. It is not industrialization that makes bureaucracy inevitable but the combination of industrialization and particular values. It is because of the mix of setting and priorities, not because of the setting alone, that we have bureaucracy as the dominant form of social organization. I shall return to this point in the last chapter, by which time the particular configuration of setting and priorities that produced bureaucracy should be clear.

My thesis about bureaucracy suggests an answer to the

third question I raised, concerning the interconnections between the dimensions of educational structure or, as we now
might phrase it, between bureaucracy and social class. We
know that education is bureaucratically organized; we know
that it reflects class bias in its purposes and operations. Are
the two features independent, at least in their origins if not
in their present form? The answer is no. Bureaucracy came
about because men confronted particular kinds of social problems with particular social purposes. Those purposes reflected
class attitudes and class interests. Modern bureaucracy is a
bourgeois invention; it represents a crystallization of bourgeois social attitudes. To its founders, as I hope the book will
make clear, the purposes of the school system and its structure were clearly interrelated. They understood that part of
the message they wished to have transmitted, the attitudes
they wished formed, would inhere in the structural arrangements themselves rather than in explicit didactic procedures.
What they did not admit, although it is hard to see how they
could have failed to realize it, was that the bureaucratic structure, apparently so equitable and favorable to the poor, would
in fact give differential advantage to the affluent and their
children, thereby reinforcing rather than altering existing patterns of social structure. Through bureaucracy, the myth of
equal opportunity has been fostered, while the amount of
social mobility has been strictly regulated.

Once more we have clues to the answer to the next question: Why has the structure of American education remained
impermeable to reformist thrusts? Part of the answer, of
course, is that the structure serves powerful interests. It serves
the interests of the educators by providing career-lines and
regulating entry. They have no intention of permitting its alteration now, and they had none a century ago, as the example of Boston presented later in this book makes clear. The
structures serve the interest of affluent groups, too, by working
in favor of their children and giving them a disproportionate

share of public funds. For those who control the system there has been no point in making fundamental structural alterations.

That is one reason the system has remained unreformed. Another is that very few people, until now, have seriously tried to change it. The reforms that have been proposed at various times, and frequently even enacted, generally consist of moving around the objects in the box, to return to my earlier image. I include in this description the reformers of the progressive period of the late nineteenth century, as I shall explain in the last chapter. Additionally, reformers have proceeded with an ineptitude of thought and strategy that has doomed their efforts from the very start. They have ignored the sociological constraints that impede changes within organizations and have lacked the strength or courage to think through the logic of their criticisms. Sometimes they have disturbed the equilibrium of a system for a few years, but in most cases it has reasserted itself, allowing things to continue pretty much in their old way. One clear instance of that was the abortive reform movement of the late 1870's in Boston, which is described in some detail in Chapter 2.

With the foregoing in mind, we can answer what to me seems a critical question confronting contemporary reformers: Must structural change precede educational change? Or is it possible to alter the purposes, biases, and actual functioning of schools without at the same time changing, radically, the structures through which they are organized and controlled? If my reading of history is roughly accurate, the answer to the second question is no. Forms of organizational structure are not and cannot be neutral. The relationships between bureaucracy, class bias, and racism are fixed. They emerged together a century ago, and they have remained essentially unchanged ever since. To attack one without the other would seem to be, if I am right, at best a waste of time and at worst another diversion from the serious need for social and educational reform within American society. Such is the message of this book.

Some will argue that this book is unduly presentist and that it twists the past in the service of contemporary positions on social issues. No historian can entirely divorce the categories with which he approaches the contemporary world from those with which he studies the past. Our concerns shape the questions that we ask and, as a consequence, determine what we select from the virtually unlimited supply of "facts." That state of affairs remains submerged and implicit in most historical work. In this case I have chosen to make manifest my questions and my concern. The concern is to provide a perspective that will be helpful in understanding and, I hope, improving urban education today.

Sociological concepts have been indispensable in forming that perspective, and I have used them deliberately and explicitly. The systematic use of concepts and the application of intellectual constructs give explanatory power to history, for they permit the formation of general statements. Too much historical work, however, continues to be remarkably unanalytical. It rests, for instance, on ideas about motivation that are quaint in terms of contemporary behavioral theory. It speaks of institutions and groups as if theories of society, organization, and stratification did not exist. As a consequence, written history usually offers no general statements that can be tested in different settings; it approaches data in a method so unsystematic that its findings cannot be replicated.

In short, there is little on-going, substantive discourse that permits historians to build on one another's work in any but the most primitive sense of adding more facts or extending the chronology backward or forward in time. It seems to me that the time for methodological unconsciousness within history has ended. Narrative history, uninformed by social or behavioral science, is pleasant and sometimes even interesting, but as a way of either advancing knowledge or contributing to substantive intellectual problems it is virtually useless.

Significant problems do not respect disciplinary boundaries; that is true for both intellectual and practical issues. Disciplines are constructs invented for the convenience of academics. They serve a useful function as a way of inducting new research workers into problems and providing an initial orientation to issues, but they should not be taken too seriously. The relations of structure and purpose in organizations, of bureaucracy and social class in education—these are not historical questions or sociological ones or some curious amalgam of the two. They are important intellectual problems that involve the past and the present, and they should be regarded in that light. Social science cut off from its historical base, as Robert Nisbet has elegantly demonstrated in *Social Change and History* (Oxford University Press, 1969), has weaknesses as grave as those of historical writing uninformed by social theory. The same can be said of social reform uninformed by history, which too often rests largely on myth. Myth, in turn, inhibits change by attaching sentimental or unreal value to institutions and forms that should be discarded.

History can serve reform partly by emancipating it from dependency upon an idealized past; it can help develop the strength of will and clear judgment that come from an ability to confront both past and present as they actually exist. That is a major purpose of this book. For we have many myths about education. We imagine educational arrangements that once were warm, democratic, and communal; we see the schools of long ago as providing a solid training in basic skills and opening up countless avenues of social mobility. We cast a rosy glow over the educational past and too often seek a restoration. But that image is a regressive fantasy and nothing more, as I hope this book will make clear.

Class, Bureaucracy, and Schools

1

Alternative Proposals for American Education: The Nineteenth Century*

There are no effective alternatives in American life. This is a realization to which the young came first and older reformers more slowly. The creation of a counterculture and the attempt to find alternatives to public schooling express the same impulse and the same truth. There is only one way to grow up in America if one wants to eat regularly, to be warm, and not to be harassed by the police. For the vast majority there is only one place to go to school, and that place is the same nearly everywhere. There is one city, one mode of production, one road to power. And there is little freedom. The essence of freedom resides in choice, and for most of us the range of

* A fully documented version of this chapter can be found in my article "From Voluntarism to Bureaucracy in American Education," *Sociology of Education*, Summer, 1971. This material is adapted and reprinted by permission of the American Sociological Association. Citations for quotations can be found in my *The Irony of Early School Reform: Educational Innovation in Mid-Nineteenth-Century Massachusetts* (Cambridge: Harvard University Press, 1968; reprinted by Beacon Press, 1970).

options in anything grows smaller. The uniformity shaped in the name of the public weal is a bankrupt social policy. It engenders a sense of overwhelming futility; there is no reason to work for change. Meanwhile, every serious social problem increases in scope and severity from year to year, and traditional approaches to social reform offer nothing very new.

This is why the search for alternative social policies has caught the imagination of workers in every field. It is the last hope. But although devising alternatives may be a nice intellectual game, creative and socially conscious, it can be no more than that—a fashionable and decadent exercise, a way of playing the fiddle while America burns. To go beyond that and inject realism into intellectual play is by no means easy. For there is a congruence between the rigid, centralist character of American life and its social and industrial structures. The weight of intellectual argument is, in fact, on the side of the proponents of inevitability, who argue that hard-headed acceptance of contemporary forms is the only way an advanced industrial society can manage its business, both public and private. That is the moral of functional social science.

It is a moral that many of us would rather not accept; to reject it, however, we must answer a very difficult question. Is it possible—in a fashion totally devoid of romantic posturing—to imagine a way in which things might be different, and a way in which that difference might be brought about? In the American past some people answered that question affirmatively. They did not answer it very well, for they failed, and they failed so completely that their efforts remain obscured by history. In the usual picture, historical development refers to the emergence of the forms we now have; the possibility that we might have had others, the serious challenge of alternative models, remains unexplored. But such exploration is of significance; it offers at least the knowledge that some people did not think that the present, as we know it, was inevitable. Their failures provide case studies for contemporary proponents of alternatives.

Nineteenth-century Americans did not have well-established forms of social organization to attack. Consequently, they expressed their alternative visions as they self-consciously built a society. In fact, the creation of institutions preoccupied early-nineteenth-century Americans. Whether they were building banks or railroads, political parties or factories, hospitals or schools, Americans confronted the inappropriateness of traditional European organizational arrangements, and their attempts to find a suitable fit between the form and the context of social life stimulated a prolonged national debate. For the most part, the public record of that controversy rests in massively tedious proposals for the introduction or alteration of particular organizational details; it appears to be the prosaic and even trivial account of practical men solving everyday problems. Yet, the arguments of those practical men over the external features of institutions frequently represented a fundamental clash of social values. The task of appropriately arranging public activities formed an intimate part of the problem of building a nation, and alternative proposals embodied different priorities and dissimilar aspirations for the shape of American society.

Four major alternatives, four models of organization, conflicted in the first half of the nineteenth century. This chapter delineates those models with the data of educational history; the final chapter points to their echoes in the contemporary search for alternatives to public education and in current reform proposals. I call the four models paternalistic voluntarism, democratic localism, corporate voluntarism, and incipient bureaucracy.

In the nineteenth century, as now, the controversy over the shape of education reflected a debate over the shape of society.

Thus the analysis of organizational models, of alternative proposals, provides direct insight into the key value conflicts within American culture.

The above observation poses a theoretical problem of major importance: what formulation best describes the varying relationships among social change, social structure, and organizational form? I shall return to the question later and argue, briefly, that organizations derive their peculiar importance from their position as mediators between social change and social structure. I shall try, in the process, to demonstrate a connection between bureaucracy and social class. Bureaucracy is not a neutral form; it represents the crystallization of particular social values. In America those values have expressed, and worked for, class interests.

An initial caution about the four models is in order: They are not ideal types. Real and fully developed instances of each can be located. However, that is not to say that in all, or even most, cases pure and unadulterated forms existed. On the contrary, organizational forms often had features of more than one model, although in such instances the features of one were almost always dominant and provided the tone. In the first part of the analysis that follows I shall discuss pure instances of each model. Later I shall return to the problem of overlap.

For the most part, the debate centered on objective questions—that is, definite structural characteristics on which organizations may be said to differ. The primary dimensions in controversy were scale (or size), control, professionalism, and finance. Each proposal concerning one of these organizational characteristics rested on social values, which, although often remaining implicit, had enormous emotional significance. (We have only to recall the decentralization controversy in New York today to realize the emotionally laden value content of issues of control and professionalism in education.) At the same time, issues of value often explicitly enveloped the debate, especially when the proponents raised questions of organizational purpose. And here the issue most frequently in dispute became the degree of standardization that was desirable in American institutional forms, behavior, and cultural values.

Paternalistic Voluntarism

The New York Public School Society represents the paradigm of paternalistic voluntarism in educational organization. Established as the New York Free School Society in 1805, it stated its purpose as "extending the means of education to such poor children as do not belong to, or are not provided for by, any religious society." The Society offered poor children training in the rudiments of literacy and in morality as it unabashedly tried "to counteract the disadvantages resulting from the situation of their parents." Despite its use of the term "free school," it should be noted, the Society did not advocate tax-supported education in our contemporary sense. Rather, it promoted free schooling only for the very poor.

For almost twenty years, the Society's members aimed but to be "humble gleaners in the wide field of benevolence," touching only the unchurched poor, "such objects . . . as are left by those who have gone before." However, by 1825 the Society had reversed its goal and argued that "it is totally incompatible with our republican institutions, and a dangerous precedent" to allow any portion of the public money to be spent "by the clergy or church trustees for the support of sectarian education." The organization had come to this position partly through participating in an acrimonious controversy involving the alleged misappropriation of educational funds by the Bethel Baptists, who, it was charged, used their share of the state education grant to build a church rather than a school. The interdenominational bickering that resulted convinced the Society that only the establishment of a single nonsectarian educational agency for the entire city could "pre-

vent strife and jealousy and preserve the harmony which has
heretofore so happily existed between the several religious societies in this place."

The generally low quality of small private schools and the
evident dissatisfaction of many parents with existing school
facilities combined to bolster the Society's claim that a major
reorganization of education within New York City had become imperative. Never modest, the Society proclaimed itself
the most appropriate agency to assume the task of educating
all the city's children, offering in support of its claim "an experience of nineteen years, during which period it has educated more than twenty thousand of our poor children." The
legislature accepted the claim of the Society, which became
the New York Public School Society and, as such, began to
disburse virtually the entire public grant for elementary education in the City of New York.

Throughout both phases of its history, voluntarism underlay
the organization of the Society, which was administered by
an unpaid, self-perpetuating board of first citizens who, "having a desire to serve mankind, associate together" and "offer
themselves to the public as agents to carry out certain benevolent purposes," doing so " 'without money and without
price' " as "servants" of the people. It was precisely this fact,
the unrewarded and disinterested dedication of "that class of
men" found in "large cities . . . having leisure and . . . benevolent feelings, who may not wish to mingle in the contest
of politics . . . but who desire to devote themselves to some
good and benevolent objective . . . and in a quiet way accomplish something for the benefit of mankind"—the enlist-
ment of the energy of this class of distinguished citizens, who
would not stoop to practice democratic politics—that gave this
form of organization its distinctive virtues in the eyes of its
champions.

The Society exemplified voluntarism, and therein lay the
source of its success: "All experience *will* demonstrate, that

public objects are better accomplished by these voluntary servants, than they are usually accomplished by persons chosen directly by the people." Voluntarism in practice embodied honesty and zeal. Between 1813 and 1840 the Society spent more than $1 million and "like faithful servants . . . accounted for every cent." In the process of distributing funds, the Society's members had revealed an enthusiastic interest in the cause of education that no paid agent could ever match; during a representative year they "themselves visited the schools *eleven thousand times*." "Point out to me," challenged a Society champion, "your school commissioners who, receiving pay, have done such service." And, he asked a basically hostile audience, "will you, as wise men, say we shall avail ourselves of these voluntary services, or shall we mingle every thing in the turmoil of politics?"

To the supporters of the Public School Society, voluntarism remained a variety of *noblesse oblige*; it rested on faith in the individual talented amateur and, at an over-all administrative level, scorned the need for elaborate organization, state control, or professional staff. As its defenders pointed out, from at least one perspective paternalistic voluntarism worked extremely well. With minimal administrative expense, scrupulous financial integrity, and commendable efficiency, the society maintained for decades an extensive network of schools that taught thousands of children a year.

But make no mistake about it: This was a class system of education. It provided a vehicle for the efforts of one class to civilize another and thereby ensure that society would remain tolerable, orderly, and safe. To the Society, the alarmingly low level of school attendance reflected "either . . . the extreme indigence of the parents . . . or their intemperance or vice; or . . . a blind indifference to the best interests of their offspring." Thus nurtured in "ignorance and amidst the contagion of bad example," these urchins, "instead of being useful members of the community, will become the burdens and pests of society." One method of class civilization employed by the Society was the instruction of parents through public addresses, in which the poor were admonished to "use all endeavors to preserve [their children in] innocency" and to practice temperance, industry, piety, frugality, and, of course, cleanliness, without which "your enjoyments as well as your reputation will be impaired."

But the schools themselves obviously constituted the major agency of class civilization. Within the schools, the particular form of pedagogy applied clearly reflected the Society's goals and its perception of its clients. The Society offered mass education on the cheapest possible plan, the monitorial or Lancasterian system, which counterbalanced a lack of central organization with rigid internal arrangements for each school. In this system, one master instructed a number of older pupils, who, in turn, taught younger ones carefully prescribed lessons. Discipline was strict, based often on shame and the use of humiliating punishments. Competition among students was keenly promoted. The schools were enormous one-room affairs, often with several hundred students and only one master. As De Witt Clinton put the case enthusiastically in 1809, the Lancasterian system "is, in education, what the . . . machines for abridging labor and expense are in the mechanic arts." The system arrived "at its object with the least possible trouble and at the least possible expense." Aside from its minuscule cost per pupil, this mechanistic form of pedagogy, which reduced education to drill, seemed appropriate because the schools served lower-class children who could without offense be likened to unfinished products, needing to be inculcated with norms of docility, cleanliness, sobriety, and obedience.

In Lancasterian schools, "solitary study" did not exist; children were "taught in companies." Teachers and monitors worked to instill "constant habits of attention and vigilance," and an "ardent spirit of emulation [was] kept continually alive. . . . The discipline of the school is enforced by shame, rather than inflicted by pain." It is not difficult to see a very particular ideal of an urban working class implicit in those pedagogical arrangements. As a result of such schooling, the working class would be alert, obedient, and so thoroughly attuned to discipline through group sanctions that a minimum of policing would ensure the preservation of social order. But, and this is important, programmed from an early age to compete with one another, working-class children would not grow up to form a cohesive and threatening class force. The zealous amateurs of the New York Public School Society, it thus becomes apparent, did not design their system for their own children or for the children of their friends. Rather, they attempted to ensure social order through the socialization of the poor in cheap, mass schooling factories.

Critics of paternalistic voluntarism stressed three defects. First, it devolved "upon a private corporation the discharge of an important function of government, without a direct and immediate responsibility to the people." In that respect it was undemocratic and exemplified "a principle . . . hostile to the whole spirit of our institutions." The basis of the democratic theory of public organizations was a belief in the "competency" of the people "to manage all the affairs of government." Thus, to deny them the ability to "determine on the mode, manner, and extent of instruction to be given to their offspring" amounted to overturning "the foundation of our whole system."

More than that, according to its critics, the New York Public School Society was "not a *voluntary system*, in the fullest and broadest meaning of the term." The plan of the Society perverted the notion of voluntarism, because it assumed "exclusive control" of children without permitting their parents any participation whatsoever in "the direction of the course of studies, the management of the schools or . . . the selection of teachers." The Society ordered parents, with "no action or cooperation," to "submit their children to the government and guidance of others, probably strangers, who are in no way accountable to those parents."

The attack on the antivoluntarist nature of the Society signaled a shift in the meaning of voluntarism, which by the 1840's in the American context no longer found favorable expression through *noblesse oblige*. By then, voluntarism had come to mean willingly offered participation in the conduct of institutions owned and managed by elected public representatives. In one sense, the repudiation of paternalistic voluntarism was part of the general attack on monopolies that characterized public discourse in Jacksonian America.

According to its critics, paternalistic voluntarism ignored the variety of American life and reflected an unacceptable cultural bias by imposing uniform services upon a diverse clientele. Although it was often couched in religious terms, the criticism showed a perception of important cultural differences of which religious doctrines served as symptoms. To the opponents of the Society, religious differences represented one form of cultural variation toward which a democratic state had to remain neutral. Therein rested a dilemma: Schools were culturally sensitive institutions; by definition, they touched the areas of irreconcilable difference between denominations. The result was an inverse relation between the size of the school system and the degree of satisfaction it could offer its clientele. It was in that respect, critics argued, that the advantage lay with county school districts, in which small and relatively homogeneous groups controlled and shaped local schools to suit their own preferences. Here, too, lay the defect of the New York Public School Society, which, simply because of the scale of its operation, could never satisfy the various publics of New York City. The defect, critics made clear, inhered not in the peculiarly insensitive behavior of the Society so much as in faults endemic to large organizations. "The defect is one which, so far from being peculiar to the Public School Society, is necessarily inherent in every form of organization which places under one control large masses of discordant materials, which, from the nature of things, cannot submit to any control." An educational agency that could not adapt to the variety of urban life, from this point of view, clearly violated the criteria for free and democratic institutions.

Animosity toward upper-class benevolence underscored both religious and political denunciations of paternalistic voluntarism. A Catholic spokesman, Bishop Hughes, argued that the class bias inherent in the New York Public School Society alienated poor Catholic children and their parents. To the assertion that the schools had the confidence of all classes, Hughes countered that the Society had been so ineffective in overcoming the reluctance of poor parents to send their children to its schools that it had applied for "a legal enactment . . . to compel an attendance." Class resentment, as much as religious resentment, underlay Hughes's bitter observation that the Society had obtained "two enactments from the Common Council, depriving the parents, in time of need—even when cold and starvation have set in upon them—of public relief, unless the children were sent to those or some other schools." So concerned with the problem of attendance had the Society become that it urged "ladies . . . to obtain [the] confidence [of the poor] by soothing words" and "employers to make [school attendance] the condition of employment." "Yet, after all this," Hughes scoffed, "they pretend that they have the confidence of the poor."

Bourgeois hostility toward paternalistic voluntarism bore a relationship to working-class antagonism. Through the existence of organizations such as the Public School Society, free education, public education, and the monitorial system had all become identified with lower-class education. When a New Jersey teacher first observed the monitorial system in the 1820's, he supposed that it was "particularly appropriate to large schools of the poor." However, after studying its operation for a time, he changed his mind and returned to New

Jersey to open a monitorial school for children of all classes. "But I found the rich sent poor children to me, and withheld their own. They had the common ideas about the system." His school lasted but twelve weeks.

An attempt to dissociate public and pauper underlay the free-school movement. Pennsylvania offers a case in point: The constitution of 1790 provided free education only for the poor, and free education had thus come to be associated with charity. In the 1830's the state legislature passed permissive legislation allowing local school districts to introduce free schools for all children. When representatives to the state constitutional convention of 1837–38 tried to enshrine this principle in the revised constitution, a full-scale debate (in which the free-school forces lost) ensued. Both sides to the debate, it is important to remember, professed allegiance to the idea of universal education and the provision of education without cost to those unable to pay. But the opponents of the free-school legislation had two misgivings about the proposed legislation. For one thing, they disliked the style of imposed social change which it represented, a point to which I shall return. For another, and most relevant here, some simply could not see why the necessity of making a public declaration of poverty would deter anyone from taking advantage of a free education. It was to the insensitivity of this point of view that the free-school proponents addressed most of their arguments. One tried to describe for his colleagues how "a feeling of repugnance" accompanied a public declaration of poverty and "prevented many persons from accepting the means of education." If the people "should be educated at the public expense, only on condition that they [be] certified and recorded as Pauper," then they would surely "refuse to avail themselves of the offer."

Thaddeus Stevens, the leading Pennsylvania advocate of free schools, connected the question with middle-class pride and status anxiety, touching what may have been many a raw nerve in the dislocations of 1837. Many people with children to be educated, he pointed out, "may have seen better days—may have been unfortunate in life, and, by reason of their reduced situation and circumstances, may be unable to educate their families." "Shall we," he asked the delegates, "do nothing to allay the prejudice, which persons in this condition will almost surely entertain, against allowing their children to be educated in public schools?" By his very terminology, Stevens reached the heart of the problem; only radical reorganization could expunge the legacy of paternalistic voluntarism and divorce the concepts of public and pauper, thereby providing institutions acceptable to proud and enterprising parents of limited means.

Democratic Localism

The first alternative proposed to paternalistic voluntarism was democratic localism. Its sponsors sought to adapt to the city an organizational form current in rural areas: the district or community school. The thorough triumph of a centralized and bureaucratic form of educational organization has diverted attention from the historical significance of the democratic localists and the seriousness with which they propounded their alternative course for American education. Therefore, it is worth dwelling on a few examples.

One is the plan offered in the early 1840's by New York's Secretary of State, John C. Spencer, in his attack on the New York Public School Society. The problems of New York City, he argued, arose from a "violation" of the principle underlying education elsewhere in the state, namely, the operation of the schools by local districts in which the "whole control" of education remained "to the free and unrestricted action of the people themselves." Thus, the New York City situation could be remedied simply by making each ward of the city an independent school district, with exactly the same powers as the districts in country towns, overseen by a Board of Commissioners with strictly limited powers. Nothing in Spencer's plan, it is important to point out, would prevent a Catholic majority in a district from hiring Catholic teachers or from choosing textbooks sympathetic to their religion. Democratic localism, like all ideologies, served many functions. One was to rationalize the drive for Catholic power in much the same fashion that democratic localism today serves as a theoretical justification for black power.

The democratic localists were active in Massachusetts as well, most conspicuously in a legislative committee that, in 1840, wrote a report favoring abolition of the state Board of Education, founded in 1837 and dominated by Horace Mann as secretary. Although the Board of Education had powers of recommendation only, the committee warned that it would soon be "converted into a power of regulation" through its close association with the legislature. Even if the powers of the board were limited to collecting and diffusing information, it should be abolished because of its inefficiency compared with that of the "voluntary associations of teachers, which preceded" its existence. "In these voluntary associations a vast number of persons are interested, a spirit of emulation exists." This spirit, and with it all educational progress, would be crushed by teacher conventions called by the state.

In fact, a central Board of Education, the Committee argued, characterized European countries where governments had to compensate for "the ignorance and incapacity of the administrators of local affairs." There, especially in France and Prussia, the schools were all modeled "upon one plan, as uniform and exact as the discipline of an army." This, of course, represented the antithesis of the American idea, which assumed the competence of the people to manage their own affairs. Hence the Board of Education appeared to be "the commencement of a system of centralization and of monopoly of power in a few hands, contrary, in every respect, to the true spirit of our democratical institutions." The bureaucratic regulations of the board, moreover, created an unnecessary nuisance, forcing teachers to fill out forms when they should be teaching children. In short, the Board would fatally damage Massachusetts education by removing its mainspring: the enthusiasm generated by participatory democracy on a local level. "Any attempt to form all our schools, and all our teachers, upon one model, would destroy all competition—all emulation, and even the spirit of improvement itself."

Orestes Brownson formalized the democratic-localist point of view into a theory of governance of American society. According to Brownson, the "individual State, as well as the Union, should be a confederacy of distinct communities," in which each vital interest remained within the smallest possible unit, of which the very smallest would be the district, "which should always be of a size sufficient to maintain a Grammar School." In education the district should remain always "paramount to the State," and each individual school should be "under the control of a community composed merely of the number of families having children in it." Although Brownson pointed out that education, like other governmental affairs, would be "more efficient" in proportion to the degree of "control" by "families specially interested in it," it is clear that efficiency was not his primary objective. Nor was it the paramount concern of other democratic localists, who subordinated both efficiency and organizational rationality to an emphasis on responsiveness, close public control, and local involvement.

Democratic localists fought, actually, on two fronts: against paternalistic voluntarism, as in their opposition to the New York Public School Society, and against bureaucracy or centralization as well, as in their attack on the Massachusetts Board of Education. Emphasis on the virtues of variety, local adaptability, and the symbiotic relation of school and community permeated both conflicts. In their resistance to bureaucracy, however, two other aspects of the democratic-localist attitude emerged most strongly. One was antiprofessionalism. The localists, unlike the sponsors of the New York Public School Society, were not vaguely indifferent to the concept of the professional educator; they were, instead, hostile and suspicious. Brownson played on the theme that normal schools (which had been introduced quite recently) were a Prussian importation to raise the specter of a cadre of Whiggish teachers learning and then imposing state-defined doctrines. "As soon as they can get their Normal Schools into successful operation," he warned, "they will so arrange it, if they can, that no public school shall be permitted to employ a teacher" not trained in one. Then, goodbye to "all liberty of instruction . . . adieu then to republicanism, to social progress."

Like Brownson, the legislative committee recommending abolition of the Board of Education dismissed normal schools as European institutions unsuited to a free society and destructive of the progress that came from the rivalry of academies and high schools vying to produce the best teachers for common schools. To this the committee added scorn for the whole idea of professional instruction for teachers: "Every person, who has himself undergone a process of instruction, must acquire, by that very process, the art of instructing others"; teachers needed special schools no more than mechanics did. Nor was it desirable to raise the job of school teaching to a "distinct and separate profession," inasmuch as schools were open only three or four months a year. "We may as well have a religion established by law," wrote Brownson, "as a system of education, and the government educate and appoint the pastors of our churches, as well as the instructors of our children."

To the democrats the threat of a state educational apparatus was the essential fault in the centralizing viewpoint: the willingness to impose social change and to force attitudes upon the people. An advocate of a local option system for education in Pennsylvania stressed that it was more important even than the existence of free schools to "adapt the system, as nearly as possible, to the *wishes,* as well as the *wants* of the people. No project, however beneficial may be its anticipated operation, should be forced upon the community by other inducements, than those arising from its own merits." Ultimately, this point of view reflected a faith in the wisdom of the people: "Any system perfectly fitted to the wants of society, cannot long remain unpopular," whereas to force innovation upon the community prematurely "can only produce evil, as it may be the means of preventing the general spread and adoption of a system, intrinsically beneficial." A delegate to the state constitutional convention pinpointed the desire to compel the maintenance of free schools by "gentlemen" who believed that "the mass of the people are not intelligent enough to act upon the subject themselves."

The case of the democratic localists, then, rested ultimately on a combination of faith in the people and a point of view about the sources of social change. "If we ever expect to root deeply this system in the affection of the people," warned a delegate to the Pennsylvania convention, "we must make the system voluntary—entirely so. But if we force it upon the people, it will be taken with an ill grace, and will be made use of, if used at all, with reluctance and suspicion." To the democratic localist, legislatures should enact, not lead, the public will. If a large minority happened to oppose a solution, however desirable the outcome might seem, it would be folly to legislate until the people had changed their minds. In Pennsylvania, in the last analysis, the most important legislative consideration remained the fact that "the prejudices against this system of education are very strong." The imposition of social change would never work; changes in society, in habits and in attitudes, came only from within the people themselves as they slowly, haltingly, but surely exercised their innate common sense and intelligence. By being left to their own devices, by perhaps being encouraged, cajoled, and softly educated, but not by being forced, the people would become roused to the importance of universal education and the regular school attendance of their children.

As a proposal for the organization of urban education (for instance, one scheme put forward for New York City), democratic localism flourished for only a short time. Its failure was predictable from the start, for it rested on a distinctly rural point of view. Its proponents did not adapt their viewpoint to the city and hence ignored critical differences between rural and urban contexts and the special problems the latter posed for the conduct of education, points to which I shall return. Nor did its sponsors—for instance, Berkshire Congregationalists in Massachusetts—see the ironically undemocratic possibilities inherent in giving free rein to local majorities.

Democratic localism referred at once to an intellectual construct and a real situation. Its problem was the lack of congruence between the two. As an intellectual construct, it offered a simple explanation and a simple cure for feelings of powerlessness and dislocation induced by the rapid social change of the 1830's and 1840's. But, unfortunately, it rested on a nostalgic memory whose relationship to reality was, at best, problematical. For was the small rural town the warm, enlightened, coherent exemplar of democracy that romantic intellectuals would have us believe? Certainly, at its worst, democratic localism in action was the tyrannical local majority whose ambition was control and the dominance of its own narrow sectarian or political bias in the schoolroom. Orestes Brownson notwithstanding, the people of the Berkshires probably concerned themselves more with the problem of putting orthodox texts into the classroom than with the theory of federalism. Whatever John C. Spencer believed, democratic localism at one level rationalized the Catholic desire to run Catholic schools with public money. More often than its theoretical exponents would care to admit, the reality of democratic localism came closer to the Hoosier School Master than to Brownson's portrait. Walking into Flat Crick, Indiana, in search of a teaching job, Ralph Hartsook confronted one of the local trustees, "old Jack Means":

> "Want to be a school-master, do you? Well, what would *you* do in Flat Crick deestrick, *I'd* like to know? Why, the boys have driv off the last two, and licked the one afore them like blazes. . . . They'd pitch you out of doors, sonny, neck and heels, afore Christmas. . . .
>
> "You see," continued Mr. Means, spitting in a meditative sort of way, "you see, we a'n't none of your saft sort in these diggins. It takes a *man* to boss this deestrick. Howsudever, ef you think you kin trust your hide in Flat Crick school-house, I ha'n't got no 'bjection. . . . Any other trustees? Wal, yes. But as I pay the most taxes, t'others jist let me run the thing."

Nevertheless, despite its intellectual softness, democratic localism at its best provided a noble alternative vision: It embraced a broad and humanistic conception of education as uncharacteristic of nineteenth-century as of twentieth-century schools and schoolmen. Consider, for example, Brownson's exhortation, which eschewed the specially utilitarian in education in terms of a distinctively American social structure:

> Here professions and pursuits are merely the accidents of individual life. Behind them we recognize Humanity, as paramount to them all. Here man, in theory at least, is professor. Professions and pursuits may be changed according to judgment, will, or caprice, as circumstances permit, or render necessary or advisable. Consequently, here we want an education for that which is permanent in man, which contemplates him as back of all the accidents of life, and which shall be equally valuable to him whatever be the mutations which go on around him, the means he may choose or be compelled to adopt to obtain a livelihood.

The education of importance thus was "general education" or the "education of Humanity," education that "fits us for our destiny, to attain our end as simple human beings."

Corporate Voluntarism

A third model, coexistent with paternalistic voluntarism and democratic localism, was corporate voluntarism, the conduct of *single* institutions as individual corporations operated by self-perpetuating boards of trustees and financed either wholly through endowment or through a combination of endowment and tuition. Corporate voluntarism characterized primarily secondary and higher education, academies and colleges. As is the case with democratic localism, the victory of the public secondary school as we know it today obscures the seriousness with which many nineteenth-century educational promoters considered corporate voluntarism as an alternative model. In fact, for a time it appeared as though corporate voluntarism in the shape of academies would become the general pattern for secondary education.

Between the late eighteenth and early nineteenth centuries, the academy became the dominant institution for secondary education throughout the country. In certain ways the academy represented little that was novel. Private schools had existed throughout most of the colonial period. Some taught classical studies; others provided the only formal source of more directly vocational education, particularly in surveying, navigation, and bookkeeping, as well as English grammar and mathematics. The curricular novelty of academies rested on their combination of the two sorts of studies, classical and modern, in the same school. Administratively, the novelty of the academy lay in the wide diffusion of a particular form of organization, which had existed earlier in only a limited number of instances; this was the corporate form. The more permanent and larger academies throughout the country generally began with boards of trustees who raised money, hired a schoolmaster, obtained incorporation by the state, and continued as general managers and overseers of the school.

States accepted the corporate form of organization for secondary education as desirable public policy and actively promoted its diffusion through grants of land or money to individual academies. States conceived of academies as public institutions; in the early republican period, "public" implied the performance of broad social functions and the service of a large, heterogeneous, nonexclusive clientele rather than control and ownership by the community or state. In this respect, the policy of Massachusetts is particularly instructive, because it represents so radical a departure from the active promotion of grammar-school maintenance by towns, which had been the practice in the seventeenth and earlier eighteenth centuries.

A committee of the legislature recommended in 1797 that the state use land grants to promote the establishment of academies in each county; proponents of the measure argued that by assisting and encouraging incorporated academies the state could fulfill its obligation to ensure the existence of facilities for secondary education. Consequently, Massachusetts began a system of land grants to academies that lasted well into the nineteenth century. As late as 1838, similar arguments launched the state of Pennsylvania on an active campaign of academy assistance. These examples reveal the inadequacy of any sharp dichotomy between public and private in the early nineteenth century. Although managed and owned by self-perpetuating boards of trustees, academies were profoundly public institutions.

The policy of public encouragement and the corporate form marked academy development throughout the country. However, to ascribe very much unity to the academy movement or to academy features is misleading. As the name "academy" became fashionable, standards for its application progressively loosened until it covered most of the small, very private, and often transient schools, which far outnumbered incorporated academies. Similarly, other generalizations break down: Academies were not entirely urban or rural, boarding or day, denominational or secular. Denominations actively established academies as well as colleges, and ministers took a prominent role in their promotion and also as academy masters. The academy curriculum likewise virtually defies generalizations. Some academies stressed college preparation and hence classical studies; most included English studies as well; and many offered a secondary education to youth bound for an immediate career in commerce rather than college. The actual curricula themselves consisted of dazzling varieties of specific subjects.

The diversity that colors every aspect of an academy portrait leaves a great many questions. Hard data on a number of critical issues, such as the social background of students and the role of academies in social mobility, are lacking. Any explanation of the remarkable proliferation of academies and of their significance must be tentative at this juncture. From the point of view of state legislatures, academies must have appeared to be delightfully inexpensive and administratively simple; without the need to raise taxes, a relatively small public investment ensured the maintenance of substantial numbers of secondary schools. The tasks of founding, managing, and supervising the schools, moreover, rested with self-contained boards of trustees and thus added insignificantly to the burdens of the state. The corporate mode of control was congruent with contemporary arrangements for managing other forms of public business. As states turned from mercantilist regulation of the economy, they adopted a liberal stance that identified the public interest with unrestricted privileges of incorporation and removal of regulations governing economic activity. The argument that autonomous, competing corporations, aided but not controlled by the state, best served the public interest extended easily from finance, travel, and manufacturing to education. Academies were educational corporations.

Controversies between the supporters of academies and the advocates of public high schools provide the most explicit example of the debate over corporate voluntarism. One of the most interesting took place in 1856 and 1857 between the sponsors of the Norwich (Connecticut) Free Academy, especially the Reverend J. P. Gulliver, and the editor of the *Massachusetts Teacher*, a vigorous champion of public high schools, then more numerous in Massachusetts than in any other state. According to Gulliver, the movement for educational reform, which began in New England in the 1830's, continually encountered frustration. Especial hostility met the proposal to establish a public high school, which was defeated by the votes of the poor:

> A few (but only a few) of the heavy tax-payers were the first to smell treason. They passed the word to a set of men, who flourish in their own esteem, by exhibiting their powers in thwarting what others attempt to do. The usual cry was raised, "a school for the rich!" The prejudices of poor men were appealed to. This very class, who were to be most benefited by the change, were excited to oppose it.

Thus did the measure fail and the cause of educational improvement languish in Norwich until a group of wealthy men determined to take the initiative by uniting to "establish a high school and endow it, which should be open, free of all charge, to all classes." This they did, and the Norwich Free Academy, well financed, carefully planned, educationally progressive, opened in 1856. It was the clearest example in the country, its sponsors well knew, of an alternative to the public high school.

The sponsors of the school did not hesitate to point out the implications of its successful establishment. "There is no subject," asserted Gulliver, "which more imperatively demands

examination at the present moment than the expediency of
endowments for literary and educational purposes. The attention of men of wealth all over the country is now directed with
great interest to the subject." Gulliver had no doubt that the
Free Academy had provided a practical demonstration of the
virtues offered by endowment and essentially private management, thus setting the issue. As he made his case, Gulliver
echoed in part the champions of the New York Public School
Society when they cited its virtues:

Honesty. Never had there been reported a case of misappropriation of funds on the part of a self-perpetuating board of
trustees. *Enlightened management*. The public simply lacked
the competence to conduct secondary schools. Public discourse, said Gulliver, too often degenerated into "talk about
'popular sovereignty' and the rights of the people to manage
everything that in any way affects their interests—which is
nothing but miserable cant." After all, why not allow the
people to manage banks or insurance companies, Gulliver
asked. Or why not give to the town meeting the management
of "manufacturing corporations, benevolent societies, philan-
thropic institutions, military organizations, and ships' crews"?
Clearly, to do so would be absurd; thus it implied no denigration of the people to assert their incapacity to manage "a
school for instruction in the ancient and modern languages,
the higher mathematics, the sciences, and the fine arts." In
short, endowment lifted education out of politics and assured
it competent direction.

Edward Hitchcock, President of Amherst College, stressed a
related theme within the concept of corporate voluntarism:
the congruence between the flexibility of essentially private institutions and the variability of American conditions. Like the
democratic localists, proponents of corporate voluntarism assumed that "systems of education ought to be wisely suited to
the character and condition of the people among whom they
are introduced." From that assumption the corporate-volun-

tarist argument proceeded along two lines: "Freedom from governmental interference with our literary institutions" as a basic principle underscored the right of the parent to select his child's education, which, in turn, found expression in the establishment of academies of varying types, suited to varying tastes. To exchange this mild anarchy for a state system of secondary schools would produce a "treadmill system" that was nothing but a "wretched substitute." The other line emanating from the original premise related the individuality of the American character to the varied degrees of civilization across the country. Both arguments called for an educational system that could sensitively reflect and adequately provide for personal and cultural idiosyncrasies. One of the "excellencies" of the academies, Hitchcock submitted, was that "they can conform to all the irregular demands of society, without destroying their individuality."

Although Hitchcock may have been rationalizing low academic quality, corporate voluntarism did seem to combine the virtues of the other two models. Without the stigma of lower-class affiliation, it offered disinterested, enlightened, and continuous management that kept the operation of education out of the rough and unpredictable field of politics. At the same time, by placing each institution under a different administrative authority, it retained the limited scope essential to institutional variety, flexibility, and adaptation to local circumstance.

Academies represented the quintessence of voluntarism as *noblesse oblige*, because they rapidly diffused throughout the country a combination of public goals and private control wrapped in the mantle of disinterested service. But the emergence of a new definition of "public school" signaled the demise of corporate voluntarism as public policy. George Boutwell, one-time Governor of Massachusetts, secretary of the Board of Education, and eventually United States Senator, stated the matter with precision: "A *public school* I understand to be a school established by the public—supported chiefly or entirely by the public, controlled by the public, and accessible to the public upon terms of equality, without special charge for tuition." With great care he went on to specify why the Norwich Free Academy and similar schools could not be considered public. Although they were "sometimes, upon a superficial view, supposed to be public," schools of that sort were only "public in their use, but not in their foundation or control, and are therefore not public schools." Academies could not be considered public schools, and in the context of the times "public" had become a necessary label. Thus, as it became apparent that only institutions financed by the community or state and directly controlled by its officers merited that definition, both paternalistic and corporate voluntarism were doomed.

Incipient Bureaucracy

Among the competing organizational models, incipient bureaucracy triumphed. The promoters of bureaucracy, including the great figures of the "educational revival," like Horace Mann and Henry Barnard, concentrated on attacking democratic localism, which was the chief hindrance to their schemes. They struck first at the notion that democratic localism was in fact democratic by pointing out that it would permit 51 per cent of the local parents to dictate the religious, moral, and political ideas taught to the children of the remainder. The proponents of democratic localism erred in assuming the widespread existence of homogeneous potential units of school administration. In actuality, the variety within most communities, city wards, or neighborhoods would foster intensely political competition for control of the local school in order to ensure the propagation of particular points of view, or, at the least, the exclusion of rival ones. "If one man claimed to have his peculiar doctrines taught, why not another?" asked Horace

Mann. "Why not all?—until you would have a Babel of creeds in the same school, which a heathen would be ashamed of." Similarly, the Free School Society warned: "If religious societies are to be the only participators of the portion of the school fund for the city of New York, a spirit of rivalry will . . . be excited between different sects, which will go to disturb the harmony of society, and which will early infuse strong prejudices in the minds of children taught in the different schools." Aside from the debilitating effect of political struggle upon education, the result could easily abridge the liberties of parents by forcing them to choose between submitting their children to alien points of view and arranging for expensive private schooling.

The second defect of democratic localism was, as I have noted, a rural bias, which overlooked the special educational problems posed by cities. Population growth and heterogeneity made extremely decentralized administration inefficient in an urban setting, because the existence of "two or more independent . . . half belligerent and jealous districts" and "a double or treble set of officers" represented an uneconomical duplication of facilities and units, which would squander financial resources. Democratic localism within a city encouraged an inequitable situation as well, for it allowed a lack of parity in educational facilities and standards within a relatively small geographical area. Thus, the improvement of the "territorial and administrative agencies, and organization of our common schools so as to enable all the people of a city or borough to act on this great interest as they act on their other great interests"—an "immediate union of all the districts"—represented the "first great step" in urban school reform.

The inefficiency of democratic localism prevented the schools from undertaking the distinctive tasks assigned them in urban settings. School reformers perceived the city through an ambivalent and nostalgic lens, which registered modern life as at best a problematical substitute for the pastoral setting of early New England. Once, there had been "no cities and but few large towns"; most men lived by "agriculture and the ruder forms of mechanical labor." By contrast, the "attendants" of modern civilization were "populous cities, narrow streets, dark lanes, cellar habitations, crowded workshops, over-filled and over-heated factories, and . . . sedentary pursuits that tax and wear and destroy the physical powers, and undermine the moral and mental." With its "melancholy train of evils," civilization "is not an unmixed good; and we cannot offer to the city or the factory any adequate compensation" for the pure and healthful life "which may be enjoyed in the country villages and agricultural districts."

Whether the compensation could or could not be adequate, it was to come primarily from one source. For a complex variety of reasons (which I shall consider in Chapter 3), schools came to be perceived as the key agencies for uplifting the quality of city life by stemming diffusion of the poverty, crime, and immorality that were thought to accompany urban and industrial development. As Henry Barnard phrased the problem: "The condition and improvement of her manufacturing population, in connection with the education of the whole people, is at this time the great problem for New England to work out." Schools had to halt the impending degeneracy of the New England character and heal the developing class gulf within New England cities, where existed "poverty, ignorance, profligacy, and irreligion, and a classification of society as broad and deep as ever divided the plebian and patrician of Ancient Rome."

In that setting, the first problem of the schools became, very simply, to ensure the regular attendance of all children upon a prolonged, systematic, and carefully structured formal education. Within the city, "so unfavorable" were the "surrounding circumstances," so "numerous . . . the temptations in the

street, from the example and teaching of low-bred idleness"
that school attendance should begin at the age of five. In fact,
the incompetence of the urban poor as parents implied the
need to exchange the natural for an artificial family setting:

> No one at all familiar with the deficient household arrange-
> ments and deranged machinery of domestic life, of the extreme
> poor, and ignorant, to say nothing of the intemperate—of the
> examples of rude manners, impure and profane language, and
> all the vicious habits of low bred idleness, which abound in
> certain sections of all populous districts—can doubt, that it is
> better for children to be removed as early and as long as pos-
> sible from such scenes and examples.

As might be expected from their image of the urban poor,
school reformers held that "the primary object" in removing
the child from the influence of the parent to the influence of
the school was "not so much . . . intellectual culture, as the
regulation of the feelings and dispositions, the extirpation of
vicious propensities, the preoccupation of the wilderness of
the young heart with the seeds and germs of moral beauty,
and the formation of a lovely and virtuous character by the
habitual practice of cleanliness, delicacy, refinement, good temper, gentleness, kindness, justice, and truth." Under the influence of a surrogate mother, a female teacher, the process
should continue until the age of twelve, at which time working-class children might safely leave school to receive the rest
of their character training in the practical business of earning
a living. The matter of school attendance, warned Barnard,
was not to be taken lightly. Should its neglect continue, society would reap its "retribution" for the "crime of neglected
childhood."

Barnard, it is of great significance to remember, accurately
reflected the sentiment of most people promoting schools.
Nearly without exception, they chose the heart over the head.
Moral education, or the formation of right attitudes, was

more important than learning any skill or subject. Schools existed to serve society by tending the characters of otherwise neglected children.

That task assumed special importance in relation to industrial society. The values to be instilled by the schools were precisely those required for the conduct of a complex urban society—for example, the importance of time. Expressed as the problem of irregular and tardy attendance, the problem of instilling a sense of time into children and their parents obsessed school committees. Aside from the real problems caused by a lack of that sense, the great stress on time indicates a concern that extended beyond the schoolroom. One writer, to make that concern explicit, pointed to the parallel behavior required of the schoolboy and the working man. For both, "precision" had become a necessary habit; "regularity and economy of time" had come to mark "our community, as appears in the running 'on time' of long trains on our great network of railways; the strict regulation of all large manufacturing establishments; as well as the daily arrangements of our school duties." The connection was unmistakable; schools were training grounds for commerce. What had been "instilled in the mind of the pupil" became "thoroughly recognized by the man as of the first importance in the transaction of business."

The problem of time haunts developing societies; it is at the very heart of the transformation of agrarian habits, which do not emphasize precision and promptness, into habits consonant with city life and large-scale manufacture. Every society since the industrial revolution began has had to develop a mechanism for changing the behaviors appropriate in a traditional society into those called for by modernity. America handled that problem, the problem of industrial discipline, like so many others, through the schools. Industrialists, in fact, have not been hesitant about stating what they have wanted. That was clear, to take two instances, in the responses that Horace Mann and George Boutwell received in 1841 and

1859 when they asked manufacturers about the value of educated labor. One wrote that knowledge was secondary to
morality, and that educated workers showed "more orderly
and respectful . . . deportment," plus a greater willingness
"to comply with the . . . regulations of an establishment."
During labor disputes, the same experienced capitalist wrote,
"I have always looked to the most intelligent, best educated
and the most moral for support." It goes without saying that
it was "the ignorant and uneducated . . . the most turbulent
and troublesome" who acted "under the impulse of excited
passion and jealousy." The association of virtues was significant: Education, morality, and docility were all equated; they
formed a trinity marking a properly schooled man. If there be
any doubt on that point, consider the words of another manu-
facturer, who praised the "diligence and . . . willing acqui-
escence" of the educated who, working their way into the
confidence of their colleagues, exerted "a conservative influence" in times of labor trouble, an influence "of great value
pecuniarily and morally." The common school made company
men.

Henry Barnard's complaint of the "want of system" in contemporary education followed from his perception of the moral
importance of regular attendance. "What other business of
society," he asked, "could escape utter wreck, if conducted
with such want of system—with such constant disregard of the
fundamental principle of the division of labor?"

Thus, the first generation of urban schoolmen began by
rejecting democratic localism and argued for carefully structured systems of education. Fully developed plans for systems
of schools and elaborate architecture, curricula, and pedagogy
mark the reports and appeals of Mann, Barnard, and their
contemporaries. Their goal was to uplift the quality of public
education by standardizing and systematizing its structure and
content.

All their plans had certain characteristics in common, most

important among them centralization. This had two principal components: first, the modification and eventual elimination of the bastion of democratic localism, the district system, whereby each section of a town or city managed its own schools with a great deal of autonomy. The case against this I have considered above. The ultimate remedy was the replacement of the district by one central board of education. In most cases, however, that was politically impossible, and reformers consequently turned to an interim measure, the establishment of high schools. In Massachusetts, for example, both the law and practical considerations required the high school to be a town school, administered by the town school committee, and siphoning off students from all the districts into the one central institution. It was thus an administrative device for undercutting the power of the districts.

The first high school was Boston English, opened in 1820; by the start of the Civil War, Massachusetts had 103 high schools, or roughly one to every three towns and cities. Other states developed high schools in a sequence that reflected their social development, for high school establishment generally accompanied the diffusion of urban features and attitudes. The first high school in Pennsylvania opened in Philadelphia in 1836; in Wisconsin, in Southport, 1849; in California, in San Francisco, 1856. Wisconsin had eleven high schools in 1865; by that date probably not more than six or seven existed in California.

In most states the initial establishment of high schools preceded both enabling and compulsory legislation. The first Massachusetts law requiring towns of a certain size to maintain a high school was passed in 1827; Pennsylvania did not pass indirectly enabling legislation until 1849; the first enabling laws in Wisconsin were passed in 1856. In each of those states, legislation represented a belated recognition of what had in fact happened, as well as, in some cases, an attempt to diffuse more widely developments already under way.

From their inception, high schools were generally public institutions in our contemporary sense of the word; they were also free and offered both classical and nonclassical courses of study. Except in large cities, high schools were usually coeducational. At first, little standardization of curriculum or internal organization existed among high schools. Some offered two-, some three-, and a few four-year courses. In cities high schools were generally large enough to permit the division of students by grade and, by the 1870's, the employment of specialist teachers in a number of subjects. Likewise, little uniformity existed in the books used, material covered, or standards attained.

The grading of schools formed the second and related component of centralization. In the district system, children of all ages were taught in one room by one teacher. That is precisely what school reformers wanted to end. As Barnard put it, one of the principal "conditions of success" for a system of public schools was a "classification of scholars" that brought "a large number of similar age and attainments, at all times, and in every state of their advancement" together within classrooms under the exclusive charge of the same teacher. Reformers argued that graded schools yielded enormous increases in educational efficiency and effectiveness, and their blueprints featured carefully designed sequences of schools of which a high school formed the apex.

An emphasis on supervision accompanied centralization. The opponents of democratic localism argued eloquently for state boards of education with paid secretaries and, at the local level, for superintendents of schools. In Boston the Annual Visiting Committee in 1845 described a state of administrative anarchy—"twenty-four men, not paid for any labor, who share a responsibility, which, thus broken into fragments, presses no one"—and concluded that the system wholly lacked "permanence, personal responsibility, continued and systematic labor." These elements could be introduced quite readily through the employment of a superintendent, an adequately paid, tenured, full-time administrator. Like the grading of schools, a superintendent would improve educational efficiency and, in addition, would increase the honesty of school operation to a degree that would more than compensate for his salary.

The stress on paid, full-time supervision spilled over into arguments for professional expertise. The emphasis on teacher training and the development of normal schools became an intimate aspect of the bureaucratic strategy. The case for normal schools shared an important assumption with the argument for professional supervision: that education had become a difficult and complex undertaking whose conduct and administration required individuals with specialized talents, knowledge, and experience. As one writer stated the matter: "The man who imagines himself a teacher, qualified for the responsible duties of an instructor, merely because he has seen others teach in a particular way, is just as much an empiric, as a pretender in medicine, who occasionally walks through the wards of a hospital." The "day for quack pedagogues is passed."

Professionalism and system, like the obsession with punctuality, reflected industrial values. Newly industrialized people must learn to reward a man for what he can do rather than for who he is. They must supplant ascription with achievement. The very structure proposed for school systems expressed that goal. Graded schools, regulated promotions, and trained staff were designed to counter problems created by a populace accustomed to gaining privileges by means that had little to do with capacity to perform. Parents, for instance, applied steady pressure to gain admittance to high school for their unqualified children; others circumvented competition by using their wealth to buy advantage for their children in the form of a private education; school committeemen not infrequently gave scarce jobs to indifferently qualified relatives or friends. In short, people mobilized personal influence and pressure, the weight of their position or their money, to gain rewards that their ability could not purchase.

That simply would not do. Unlike traditional societies, with well-defined roles and rigid social structures, societies that are modernizing require a commitment to competence. It is necessary to call forth and reward achievement if specialized and technical tasks are to be performed. The transition from a pre-industrial society requires a shift in the basis of social valuation from ascription to achievement. That became one function of public education, as schoolmen again attempted to facilitate economic change through the transformation of social attitudes.

The content as well as the structure of education presented a problem: how to honor minority sensibilities while inculcating the norms required for upright and orderly social living. The official response to the problem of minority sensibility was to proclaim the school religiously and politically neutral. "The great ideal" of the common school system, Horace Mann pointed out, is "that those points of doctrine, or faith, upon which good and great men differ, shall not be obtruded into this mutual ground of the schools." In practice the schools did not become neutral, as Catholic spokesmen all knew. Protestant ministers, as David Tyack has shown, played active and important roles in common-school promotion and management, and it is in fact impossible to disentangle Protestantism from the early history of the common school, which exuded an unmistakable chauvinistic pan-Protestant tone.

The class bias of education, however, was even more pervasive than its tepid Protestant tone. A configuration of moral and cultural values best described as mid-Victorian permeated school textbooks and statements of educational objectives, such as the following one, entitled "The Necessity of Restraint." Children, lamented the author (whose basic goal, like that of other reformers, might without too much distortion be termed the extirpation of sexuality) "have not learned that present self-denial is the price at which future good is often to be obtained, and that present suffering and toil are rewarded by subsequent enjoyment. These lessons the child *must* learn." Without restraint and direction, the child would become "the victim of passion, and having no rule over his own spirits, he would be exposed to fearful moral dangers." Untamed human nature, to this frightened author, strove continually to break loose into an unbridled orgy of passionate sensual indulgence. Without restraint, "without these counterchecks upon the passions," the author asked, "what would our race be?"

Thus, sublimation became the goal of public education. In 1858, for instance, the Boston Public School Committee admonished parents that "every pure and refined pleasure for which a child acquires a relish, is to that extent, a safeguard against a low and debasing one." It became a key function of the schools to teach the substitution of higher for lower pleasures, which, from one point of view, represented a systematic attempt to diffuse sexual repression throughout society. "Passionate" and "sensual" became two of the most pejorative words in educational discourse. "Those, whose minds and whose hearts have been properly trained and disciplined by education, have control over their passions. Having cultivated a taste for simple and innocent pleasures, rather than a love for vicious excitement, their desires are awakened by objects higher than any gratification merely animal." In their objectives for education, schoolmen thus reflected a peculiarly Victorian combination of sexual and status anxiety that forms one of the least lovely aspects of nineteenth-century culture. Whether that came from their own discomfort at suspecting mass indulgence of pleasures that they themselves had painfully renounced or from a desire for social control, it was apparent that the traits of character schoolmen found necessary to fit the working class for upright urban living represented an idealized Victorian middle-class portrait of itself. It is apparent, too, that public schools represented an attempt to effect a massive and permanent desexualization of society.

Herein lies an irony: Schoolmen who thought they were promoting a neutral and classless—indeed, a *common*—school education remained unwilling to perceive the extent of cultural bias inherent in their own writing and activity. However, the bias was central and not incidental to the standardization and administrative rationalization of public education. For, in the last analysis, the rejection of democratic localism rested only partly on its inefficiency and violation of parental prerogative. It stemmed equally from a gut fear of the cultural divisiveness inherent in the increasing religious and ethnic diversity of American life. Cultural homogenization played counterpoint to administrative rationality. Bureaucracy was intended to standardize far more than the conduct of public life.

An instructive instance of the above point is a debate in Pennsylvania regarding the degree of official sanction to be given to the German language. Said one speaker, "I think . . . that we ought no longer to be divided into separate races, and by distinct languages and habits." Another put the matter even more bluntly: "I think that the whole people of the state should be amalgamated as soon as that end can possibly be accomplished." It was, after all, implicit in the "common" of "common school" that education should forge social unity by blurring cultural distinctiveness—the familiar idea of the melting pot.

What is less obvious, although closely related, is the racist implication of such a point of view. If an attitude that considers one group to be different from and inferior to another in some basic and essential fashion can be labelled racist, then we are forced to the conclusion that racist sentiment scarred the origins of public education. For it is in precisely those terms—difference and inferiority—that school people perceived lower-class children. Take, for example, this description of its task offered by the Boston School Committee:

> taking children at random from a great city, undisciplined, uninstructed, often with inveterate forwardness and obstinacy, and with the inherited stupidity of centuries of ignorant ancestors; forming them from animals into intellectual beings; and, so far as a school can do it, from intellectual beings into spiritual beings; giving to many their first appreciation of what is wise, what is true, what is lovely, and what is pure; and not merely their first impressions, but what may possibly be their only impressions.

Now, the Boston School Committee was not exceptional in its perception of immigrant children. Nor was the task it described incidental to its work. As the earlier arguments from Boutwell and Barnard make clear, the urban public school had been founded to cope with the problems of urban living, among which the threat of the urban poor had high priority. It approached this task from a racist perspective on its clientele. Thus racism, like antisexuality, is integral, not incidental, to the very structure of public education. In the course of a century, the particular object has changed from Irish Catholic to black, but the attitude remains.

It was partly to deal effectively with the problem of the urban poor that bureaucracy developed as the mode of organizing urban schools. The racism thus integral to bureaucratic structure became even more deeply entrenched, because it early acquired a functional utility as a defense of bureaucratic failure. In 1876 one commentator related an alleged decrease in the standard of educational attainment to the altered background of students. No longer did they come from rural New England families, where cultivated common sense and native intelligence were the rule. Instead, the "material" that the schools were "required to shape and polish" derived from different and inferior sources:

> A very large proportion of the pupils in our cities and populous towns come from homes utterly destitute of culture, and of the means and the spirit of culture, where a book is never seen, and reading is with the adult members a lost art, or one never acquired. There are schools in which four-fifths or more of the children are of this class. I at one time had under my supervision a school in which ninety-nine percent of the children were of foreign parentage, and hardly one of the whole from a home level with the lowest status of native-born intelligence. In such minds a sunken foundation must be laid by months or years of unpromising toil, before any portion of the work begins to appear above the surface. It seems almost impossible to give them a conception of either the uses or the pleasures of knowledge, or to lead them to that primal exercise of judgment by which two ideas are compared or combined. Even the simplest object-lessons are often unintelligible to them. Instruction can hardly be conveyed to them in terms which they can understand, and in what they attempt to learn, memory derives no assistance from association. A person of exceptional skill and patience might hope out of a single such block in the lapse of years to carve a statue; but what shall we think of the sculptor who is compelled every day to make some strokes of the chisel on forty or fifty of them?

What, indeed, but to excuse his failure? That this essentially racist excuse for educational failure is reminiscent of contemporary discourse about cultural deprivation is not an accident, for the contemporary notion is but a continuation of the old: a well-developed bureaucratic strategy for explaining educational disaster by reference to the inferiority of the pupils.

Irony and class bias emerge from the early history of the high school as well as from general statements of educational purpose. For the goals and claims of high school promoters bore only a tangential relation to the facts of high school attendance and function. High school promoters coupled arguments for centralization and general educational uplift with the assertion that public secondary schools would foster the economic prosperity of the community by attracting settlers, increasing land values, and providing properly trained recruits for higher branches of industrial and commercial employment. At the same time, the influence of the high school would radiate to the community as a whole, diffusing culture among the people. Like the common schools, moreover, high schools were expected by their advocates to gather together children of all social classes and thereby promote social harmony and justice. In the high school, poor and also middle-class parents might have an opportunity to secure the advancement of their children without paying tuition; it provided an education that would foster social mobility and insure individual prosperity in a time of bewildering economic flux. For girls, the high school offered excellent preparation for schoolteaching, the most desirable occupation to which they could realistically aspire.

What little evidence exists of an actual connection between high school attendance and middle-class employment in the mid-nineteenth century seems to indicate that the schools did offer some advantages to boys in seach of white-collar work. Unquestionably, they served girls in search of teaching jobs, and female students generally far outnumbered male. However, contrary to popular belief, in its early history the high school was not popular with the working class, which frequently viewed it as a class institution irrelevant to its own aspirations and impossible to utilize when the earnings of adolescents were needed to keep the family alive. Nor, in its early history, did the high school actively promote social mobility, social harmony, or egalitarianism. Very few poor children attended; indeed, only a very small minority of the community's children even began high school, and most of them left before graduation. It was wealthy, prestigious community leaders concerned with economic development and social integration, as well as middle-class parents concerned with mobility and educational expense, who formed the nucleus of high school promoters. In the long run, the high school replaced the academy as the dominant institution for secondary education because it offered middle-class parents a means of educating their children at public expense and keeping them home during the process. At the same time, it perpetuated the differential advantages of middle-class children and may actually have served as a social sorting device, limiting rather than promoting mobility. Certainly, in some instances, the attempt to institute a high school split a community along class lines and, ironically, fostered estrangement between school and community and between social groups, a consequence precisely opposite to the one desired and anticipated by high school suppporters.

The movement of the bureaucrats in the ante bellum period was not entirely toward order and rigid system; their proposals for the actual conduct of classes and the reform of pedagogy moved in the other direction. In this they represented the opposite of the paternalistic voluntarists, who, as we have observed, combined a relative lack of external order with a rigid internal system of teaching. To the common-school revivalists, the term "mechanical," as applied to pedagogy, was thoroughly pejorative. As they systematized the administration and grading of schools, these reformers, for a complex variety of reasons, argued for a softening of pedagogy rooted in the substitution of the arousal of interest, affection for the teacher, and internalization of the desire to learn for interpersonal competition (or "emulation") and corporal punishment as sources of motivation. As one writer stated the case, motivating children necessitated *"exciting their curiosity."* The model teacher connected "with his instruction, as far as possible, what is interesting and attractive so that the associations, formed in the minds of his pupils, will leave them in love with the subject of investigation, and in the proper time, bring them back to the pursuit with readiness and alacrity." The pupil, of course, "must be made to work; but he must work voluntarily, cheerfully, with hope." In that way, the model for the teacher-pupil relation became the relation of parent and child at its finest, both firm and affectionate.

In one other crucial way the leading figures of the educational revival did not behave like traditional bureaucrats: They did not adopt the bureaucratic ideal of personality. Neither their ideal teacher nor their ideal administrator was a gray, colorless public servant efficiently and quietly executing the public will. Quite the contrary: The model for the educational administrator came neither from business nor the military but from evangelical religion. It was not a coincidence that the period of mid-century reform was called, even at the time, the educational revival. It was to be a secular evangelism. To Horace Mann, educational reform was not a task or a necessity but—and this word constantly permeates his published and unpublished writing—a "cause." Nowhere is the evangelical impulse at the heart of the educational revival more evident than in Mann's letters of encouragement to Henry Barnard. "I rejoice," he wrote, "to learn that Connecticut is engaged in the work of education. . . . What cause can be nobler? What cause holds in its embrace so much of the well-being of the future millions? . . . I welcome you as a fellow laborer in the cause of education." Writing of his strain during the attempt to abolish the Board of Education in 1840, Mann told Barnard that he found his "consolation" in "laboring in a cause, which has my whole heart. . . . I know it is the greatest of earthly causes. It is a part of my religion that it must prevail." Not only the impulse and the language, but the style as well was evangelical. For the educational revivalists saw their mission as converting the populace, if need be town by town, to the cause of salvation through the common school. "When I took my circuit last year," Mann reported to Barnard,

"I mounted *on top of a horse*, and went Paul Prying all along
the way, and diverging off to the right or left, wherever I
scented any improvement. I believe that was substantially the
way that Peter the Hermit got up the Crusades."

The educational revivalists retained from their religious
counterparts the evangelical ideal of a moral and spiritual regeneration of American society through the moral and spiritual regeneration of individual personalities. It is this goal
that lay at the center of the new, soft, child-centered pedagogy.
It was to be a pedagogy that recognized the sterility and even
the danger of cold, purely intellectual education. Warning
that dire consequences would result "unless the heart be so influenced in the tenderness of its young growth, that goodness
becomes part of its nature," one superintendent reminded his
constituents that "heart-culture should be paramount to brain-
culture, moral culture to intellectual culture." Like evangelical
religion, education had to awaken and shape the affective side
of personality by delicately stimulating and cultivating the
emotions. Like evangelism in religion as well, education thus
had to engage the interest and affections of the child if it was
to engender a deep, personal commitment to a righteous life.

That commitment was too important, too bound up with
the future of society, to be left to chance. Consequently,
schooling had to be universal, and compulsory education followed inexorably upon the demise of democratic localism.
From one direction, abridgment of the freedom of property-
owners by compulsory taxation for school support forecast
elimination of the freedom to be unschooled. "The power
which compels the citizen to pay his annual tax for the support of schools," reasoned the state superintendent in Maine,
"should, in like manner, fill the schools with all of those for
whose benefit the contribution was made." Taxation represented a "solemn compact between the citizen and State"; the
citizen contributed in order to protect his "person" and secure

his "property." The "State compelling such contributions, is under reciprocal obligation" to compel attendance at schools. Thus compulsory education became "a duty to the taxpayer."

Proponents of bureaucracy argued that the heightened importance of education in urban society required a vast increase in the proportion of community resources devoted to schooling and the attendance of all children. At first schoolmen overlooked the logic of their perception of the poor, or they might have predicted a less than enthusiastic welcome for their reformed school systems. Instead, they expected that the poor, along with everyone else, would react with warm approval to the excellence and transparent utility of new or refurbished institutions. But only the middle classes responded with enthusiasm and regularity. School promoters tried a number of expedients to promote attendance, the most notable of which was the creation of reform schools, special compulsory institutions to mop up the residue left by the regular public schools. "For those who will avail themselves of our schools, open to every child, provision is already made," wrote a Massachusetts legislative commission in 1847. "But for those who, blind to their own interests, choose the school of vicious associates only, the State has yet to provide a compulsory school, as a substitute for the prison—it may be for the gallows." The Massachusetts Reform School at Westboro, opened the following year, represented the first form of compulsory schooling in the United States.

It soon became apparent that the reform school was too small to accommodate all those who were reluctant to attend the common schools. Nor did the various truant schools in individual towns and cities solve the problem. Thus, in 1851 Massachusetts passed the first general compulsory-education law. A serious confrontation with the realities of nonattendance in that state and others had forced school promoters to recognize the logic of their long-standing position. The Pennsylvania Board of State Charities, as an instance, came to the advocacy of compulsory education by uniting the traditional relation between ignorance and crime with equally familiar arguments about the nature of cities and city children:

> The character of great cities exerts a powerful, and often a sadly controlling influence on the country, near and remote. They may be fountains of blessing to a State, or they may be sources of wide-spread corruption, nests of iniquity, festering sores upon the body politic. The children that grow up neglected in the city do not always remain there. They may carry the pestilential influence of their vices all over the State.

Reinforcing this grave danger was the unmistakable fact that "it is precisely those children whose parents or guardians are unable or indisposed to provide them with an education . . . for whom the State is most interested to provide and secure it." It was, moreover, those children who preferred "the pleasures and license of vagabondage and truancy" for whom "education is most needed." "Clearly," reasoned the board, "it is the duty, that is, it is the highest interest of the State, to secure the education of these 'neglected children,' " and the only way to accomplish this was through compulsion.

Both compulsory education and the imposition of bureaucratic reform upon reluctant communities rested on an assumption contrary to the one at the heart of democratic localism. That became perfectly clear, for example, when Thaddeus Stevens asked the delegates to the Pennsylvania Constitutional Convention of 1837: "When statesmen come into this hall, do they suppose that they come only for the purpose of acting out the ignorance of those who sent them?" If elected by men opposed to education, must a representative "therefore set his foot down against all education"? Similarly, another delegate argued, "We were told that it was dangerous to force this system upon the people, when they are not prepared to receive it; but we never heard in any state, of the people asking for provisions on the subject of education, until they were offered." The assumption here is clear: Social change flows from the top down—always and inevitably. The function of government is to lead and to educate, not to acquiesce in public whims.

That assumption made it possible to unite a number of strands and point them in only one direction. If everyone was taxed for school support, if this was justified by the necessity of schooling for the preservation of urban social order, if the beneficial impact of schooling required the regular and prolonged attendance of *all* children, and, finally, if persuasion and a variety of experiments had failed to bring all the children into school—then, clearly, education had to be compulsory. In the crunch, social change would be imposed.

Bureaucracy retained a legacy from the organizational models that it superseded. It bowed in the direction of the democrats by accepting their redefinition of voluntarism and consequently placing educational institutions under boards that were publicly elected rather than self-perpetuating. It innovated in its rejection of a loose, personalistic style of operation in favor of organizational rationality, impersonality, and professionalism. Nevertheless, in two respects the path from paternalistic voluntarism is direct. First, bureaucracy retained the notion of a central monopoly and systematized its operation through the creation of elaborately structured schools and school systems. Second, bureaucracy continued, and even strengthened, the notion that education was something the better part of the community did to the others to make them orderly, moral, and tractable. Unfortunately, the embodiment of that idea in compulsory, bureaucratic monopolies has continued to characterize American education.

Four Models: A Comparison

Thus far I have presented distinct examples of each model. This should not obscure the fact that many organizations had features of more than one, although in most instances of overlap the characteristics of a single model predominated and provided the tone. Take as one example the Boston Primary School Committee. Until 1818 Boston had only public grammar schools, entrance to which required literacy, usually acquired in small, private, fee-charging schools; this, of course, proved a burden on the poor. In 1818, after prolonged agitation, the city established a network of very small primary schools in local neighborhoods. To manage them, the city school committee itself appointed a primary-school committee, which was composed of a trustee for each school. After its initial appointment, the primary-school committee filled vacancies in its own ranks and thus became virtually self-perpetuating. Although the committee operated under public auspices, it nevertheless represents paternalistic voluntarism, because it regarded public primary education as a charity offered to the poor through the benevolent spirit and labor of an upper class.

Another sort of overlap has contaminated the bureaucratic model: the retention of democratic localism in the form of locally elected school boards, which have continued to hold ultimate authority over fully developed bureaucracies. Whether a given locality is more democratic or more bureaucratic depends on its size. In smaller communities, direct board involvement with the schools is easier, whereas in large cities the very scale of the operation, by preventing intimate board involvement, fosters bureaucratic control at all levels. It is one of the paradoxes of American education that democratic localism remains—even within cities—the official administrative ideology, while bureaucracy remains the practice.

Not all advocates of democratic localism have accepted that model in its entirety. The feature that has encouraged the most deviation has been antiprofessionalism. Democratic localists in most places were forced to recognize the appalling quality of teaching and, despite their ideological preference, realized the need to develop professional teacher training.

Finally, on occasion proponents of bureaucracy promoted corporate voluntarism. They did so in the case of public institutions that served the entire state, or a large segment of it, rather than a single community—for instance, reform schools and normal schools. In Massachusetts, philanthropists offered money to the legislature for the establishment of reform and normal schools on the condition that the grant be matched from public funds. This act, essentially a form of endowment, stimulated the state to action in the areas of both teacher training and juvenile delinquency. Both the normal school and the reform school began with their own boards of trustees, appointed by the governor. The corporate-voluntarist tone of state activity in these areas was underlined by the appointment of a separate board of trustees for each new reform and normal school created, rather than their governance by one central body.

The precise differences among the models emerge in summary fashion if we focus briefly on the four objective dimensions—scale, control, professionalism, and finance—and compare positions on each. As for scale, both the democratic localists and the corporate voluntarists advocated smallness and held the best administrative unit to be the individual institution or, at most, a section of a town. The other two models, of course, stressed size in their definition of administrative area and recommended the entire town or city, at the least, the whole state desirably, and, in some cases, the nation. On the other hand, the two varieties of voluntarist united on the question of control, favoring essentially amateur management by boards removed from direct public surveillance. On the same question, the democrats and bureaucrats united in stressing the importance of assigning management to bodies directly responsible to, and representative of, the public. However, the bureaucrats extended this position to advocate that those public bodies delegate executive responsibility to public professionals, a proposal the democrats regarded with horror.

Neither variety of voluntarist was very much concerned with the question of professionalism. Both paternalists and corporatists assumed that, as talented, educated amateurs, they were fit to manage educational institutions. Thus, when they were in control, the question of professionalism simply did not arise. Where the democrats were indifferent, interestingly, was on the question of finance. They did not especially care whether schools were absolutely free and tax-supported or partly supported by rates (a kind of fee). In fact, if free schools meant the imposition of state authority against community will, they were absolutely opposed (as the Pennsylvania constitutional convention clearly showed). The point is that free schools, while ultimately desirable, remained subordinate on the democratic-localist scale of priorities to community self-determination. The bureaucrats, with a few notable exceptions, ardently championed free schools, which were logically necessary to their ideal of universal education. The voluntarists supported tuition for those who could pay, free education for the poor, and endowment where possible.

On the question of the social role of education, the intellectual spokesmen for corporate voluntarists and democrats retained a pluralistic and sometimes libertarian vision. As one democrat put the matter, government had as a "right no control over our opinions, literary, moral, political, philosophical, or religious." To the contrary, its task was "to reflect, not to lead, nor to create the general will." Government thus "must not be installed as the educator of the people." The democrats could see no particular virtue in uniformity. It was, after all, the same writer said, the idiosyncratic character of community schools, shaped by local parents, that gave the common school its "charm."

The paternalistic voluntarists and the bureaucrats, of course, saw education in precisely the reverse light—as leading, not reflecting, the general will and at the least shaping moral opinions. The "charm" of the common school did not especially

concern them, if indeed they ever noticed it. Basically, they
hoped for increasing standardization of institutions, practices,
and culture in American society. Safety of property, upright
behavior, a reduction in crime and welfare expenses—these
values marked both paternalists and bureaucrats as the advocates of law and order of their day. As an astute critic of the
Massachusetts Board of Education pointed out with unmerci-
ful clarity, the board viewed education as "merely a branch of
the general police" and schoolmasters as only a "better sort of
constable." The "respectable" members of the board promoted universal education "because they esteem it the most
effectual means possible of checking pauperism and crime,
and making the rich secure in their possessions." Education
thus had "a certain utility" whose measure was "solid cash
saved to the Commonwealth."

Organizational Form and Social Structure

Even if the specific models proposed in this chapter are rejected, it is my hope that the underlying argument has been
persuasive. That argument is that the analysis of organizational models provides direct insight into the key value conflicts of nineteenth-century society. In their arguments over
the details of organizations, nineteenth-century Americans revealed most clearly their aspirations and their anxieties concerning the society that they would build and bequeath. However,
if we accept the centrality of organizational form to nineteenth-
century people, we are left with an important general question: Why has the nature of organization been of such primary
importance? Was it as passionate and value-laden a subject of
controversy in other countries during the same period? I suspect that the answer is, at least insofar as England and Canada are concerned, not quite; Americans made organization
uniquely their own *national* problem. And they did so precisely
because they lacked fixed traditions and the security of ancient

forms. The search for the distinctively American in art, architecture, and government, to name but three aspects of American culture, is too well known to belabor. This nervous self-consciousness knew few boundaries; it made the creation of organizations—their forms and characteristics—an intellectual and even nationalistic issue. It thus assumed special importance in the American context.

But the question of the centrality of organization can be put in a more general context as well. Even if not quite so emotionally charged, it nevertheless was important elsewhere during the nineteenth century. In both England and Canada, for instance, problems of devising or revising institutions to cope with poverty, ignorance, and other forms of social distress enlisted enormous thought and energy in precisely the same period. The explanation of that fact requires the formulation of relationships between organizations and other key aspects of nineteenth-century society, a task outside my scope in any detailed sense. However, it is important to speculate, even briefly, on the nature of that relationship and hence on the direction the inquiry into its delineation might assume. Tentatively, therefore, I should like to advance the proposition that the importance of organization derived from its mediating position between social structure and social change.

The mediating position of organizations becomes evident from a consideration of the three broad areas that must be included in any comprehensive analysis of the nineteenth century. The first is social change, perhaps best described as industrialization and urbanization. Of the three areas, that is the one we know most about. Second are changes in social structure and demographic characteristics. We have some idea of the change in the ethnic composition of the population, of its physical distribution, of the white birth rate. We know very little, in an empirical sense, about changes in structure, particularly in the family or patterns of stratification and mobility, although a number of scholars are working on these topics. However, we can be certain that there were some changes of a fairly substantial nature, whatever they may turn out to be precisely. The third area of change is organizational, which I have sketched with regard to education in this chapter.

We can observe some relations among the three major areas of change already. Paternalistic voluntarism was the form of organization characteristic of education in the preindustrial, mercantile city. Corporate voluntarism and democratic local- ism characterized rural areas and were proposed for urban places precisely at times of transition between mercantile and industrial stages of development. Incipient bureaucracy spread with incipient industrialization. In terms of social structure, we might suggest that paternalistic voluntarism characterized a society in which stratification was based on traditional no- tions of rank and deference, rather than on class in the more modern sense. Some evidence indicates that the poor and the working classes threatened by industrialization supported democratic localism in times of technological transition. How- ever, the attempt by the middle classes to secure advantage for their children as technological change heightened the impor- tance of formal education assured the success and acceptance of universal, elaborate, graded school systems. The same result emerged from the fear of a growing, unschooled proletariat. Education substituted for deference as a source of social ce- ment and social order in a society stratified by class rather than by rank.

In each instance, the organization was at the center. It was the medium through which groups or classes organized their response to social imperatives. In short, organization mediated between social change and social structure. Hence men brought to the design of their organizations their values, their ambiva- lences, their fears, and, above all, their aspirations for the shape of American society.

Two general points about the significance of the organiza- tional debate remain to be made. First of all, it refocuses the issue in the decreasingly profitable debate between proponents of consensus and of controversy as the key to the American past. If my underlying contention is valid, men did argue over fundamental value differences, which they articulated in reference to the practical problem of organization-building. Their interchange, the competition among organization forms, and the visions they expressed did provide a dynamic of controversy to nineteenth-century history. But it is a dynamic that implies no lack of faith in Lockean liberalism, no desire to subvert the existing social order, and no lack of commitment to America. The politics of organization-building *was* the politics of value clash, but the nature of that clash is not described by conventional categories of economic or class division. Just what those categories are—how to go beyond the empirical facts of organizational form to organized systems of values and their relationship to social structure—should be, I would argue, the major goal of American social historians.

The other point of significance regards alternatives. Men did see alternatives in the American past. Those whose vision embraced a path other than bureaucracy lost. But if the present was inevitable, it did not seem so to men at the time. Perhaps if they had been that much wiser—who can say? Their failure and their vision provide, respectively and at once, enduring notes of pessimism and hope, which we cannot afford to ignore today.

2

The Emergence of Bureaucracy in Urban Education: The Boston Case, 1850–84[*]

Educational bureaucracy did not remain incipient, as we all know. It developed quickly and thoroughly within large cities and has remained entrenched there ever since. This chapter explores the processes through which that situation came about and its consequences for reform.

The New York teachers' strike of 1968 highlighted two of those consequences for urban education. First of all, the hostility between the teachers and the various elected boards underlined the historic tension between professionals and lay reformers, between educators and the amateurs who control or try to change school systems. Second, the confrontation of teachers and angry people trying to bar them from the schools dramatized the long-standing estrangement, the distance, be-

---

[*] For an extended and fully documented presentation of the material in this chapter, see the two-part article that appeared under the same title in *History of Education Quarterly*, Summer, 1968, and Fall, 1968. The substance of this article is reprinted here by permission of the *History of Education Quarterly*.

tween the school and the working-class community. The two characteristics are related; both are unintended consequences of bureaucracy.

Neither was foreseen by the proponents of incipient bureaucracy. Hindsight enables us to delineate the relationship between the kind of educational structure they proposed and the tensions that characterize city school systems today. But in their eyes the problems were not inherent in the model. It was, in fact, only in practice that the weaknesses of their approach to educational reform emerged. It is therefore necessary to look closely at the context of educational reform on the local level in order to appreciate the interaction of forces that provided the dynamic of educational history and its contemporary disasters.

Bureaucracy inhibits reform. Its potent informal organizations mobilize resistance and frequently sabotage innovations. Bureaucrats counter reformist arguments by changing their own goals, replacing earlier extravagant claims with much more limited objectives, and asserting that critics misunderstand their purposes. The changes, or goal displacements, are sincerely believed in by the bureaucrats; they provide a sense of success and a buffer against tremors of self-doubt. However, in mature bureaucracies self-doubt is minimal, for the forms of organizations work changes on the personalities of those who live within them. One effect of bureaucracy is to make bureaucrats.

Bureaucracy had produced educational bureaucrats by the third quarter of the nineteenth century. That was evident in the response of schoolmen to educational critics. It was one lesson of the major controversy that rocked the Boston school system in the 1870's.

That the battle took place in Boston at that time was no accident; similar fights were being waged throughout the country at the same time. In essence, they were skirmishes between lay reformers, disenchanted with the rigid educational organizations that had so quickly emerged out of the enthusiastic educational revival of mid-century, and the now more organized and powerful schoolmen. To understand the controversy in Boston and elsewhere, it is critical to appreciate the significance of the structural alteration in the organization of urban education during the third quarter of the nineteenth century.

For the most part, histories of education follow a long-established pattern of periodization. The "revival of education" marked the few decades before the Civil War; then came "expansion of the educational enterprise," lasting from the 1870's to the 1960's, punctuated by "progressivism," which arose with reformist vigor in the 1890's and degenerated into the child-centered school by the 1920's. The trouble with this framework is that the common word "expansion" implies an evolutionary, teleological process, increments of the same piled on top of one another. Significant changes in direction are masked, and one of the most significant is the change in the nature of school systems that was effected in most areas of the East and Midwest between, roughly, 1850 and 1875. During those years, urban school systems became, in a word, bureaucracies. Except in the South, the principle of free, tax-supported public schools had been generally accepted by the time of the Civil War, but the form and organization those schools would assume in urban America had not yet been fixed. It was the function of developments in the few succeeding decades to stamp irrevocably upon urban education the classic features of bureaucracy. To examine those years, as we do in this chapter, is to explore the origins of contemporary patterns of urban educational administration and of two related major predicaments of contemporary educational reformers—the need for alternative models of educational organization, and the divorce of school and community. Besides attempting to reveal the beginnings, this chapter suggests that bureaucratization provides a valid framework for reinterpreting a number of developments and controversies in late-nineteenth-century urban education. Urban educational bureaucracies developed with local idiosyncrasies that make each unique in some ways, but they were all responses to the same kinds of pressure. Close examination of one will therefore yield more insight than a superficial recounting of many.

The Emergence of Bureaucracy

Between 1850 and 1876 the Boston school system became a full-scale bureaucracy. Bureaucracy has come to have negative connotations, perhaps rightly so, but the intent here is to use the term first of all to denote an organization marked by certain identifiable structural features. Social scientists differ concerning the exact nature of these features. The definition offered by Carl Friedrich matched the Boston situation better than the more familiar one by Max Weber; the former is more clearly stated and stems from a comparison of relatively modern political-administrative units. "The six elements of a bureaucracy," writes Friedrich, "fall naturally into two groups. Three of them order the relations of the members of the organization to each other—namely, centralization of control and supervision, differentiation of function, and qualification for office (entry and career aspects)—while three embody rules defining desirable habit or behavior patterns of all the members of such an organization—namely, objectivity, precision and consistency, and discretion." All of the elements of bureaucracy listed by Friedrich emerged in Boston during the third quarter of the nineteenth century, as Tables 1 and 2 partially reveal.

The first element of bureaucracy identified by Friedrich, "centralization of control and supervision," was reflected in the shift from a system of diffuse supervision by more than a hundred lay officials to a small school board and full-time central administrators. "Differentiation of function," the sec-

Table 1

Structure of the Boston School System, 1850 and 1876
A. Lay Supervision

1850		1876	
School committee	24 members[a]	School board	24 members[e]
Primary school committee	73 members[b]		
Total	97	Total	24

[a] Two members elected from each of the city's twelve wards in 1850, with the mayor as ex officio chairman; changed to six elected from each ward in 1854, growing to 118 members.

[b] Appointed by, but with authority independent of, the school committee; abolished in 1855, and jurisdiction transferred to school committee.

[e] As of 1875, twenty-four members elected at large from the city; name changed from committee to board that year.

B. Professional Supervision

1850	1876	
None	Superintendent	1[a]
	Board of supervisors	6 members[b]
	Principals	48[e]
	Total	55

[a] First superintendent appointed in 1851.

[b] Position of supervisor created by legislation in 1875.

[e] Masters of grammar schools appointed principals of both their own schools and primary schools in their districts in 1866.

C. Types of Schools

	1850			1876		
	Enroll-ment	No. of Schools	No. of Teachers	Enroll-ment	No. of Schools	No. of Teachers
Primary	11,000[a]	161	164	19,221	114	423
Grammar	9,071	22	167	24,788	50	580
Latin (high school)[b]	96	1	3	355	1	18
English (high school)[c]	165	1	5	483	1	20
Girls (high school)[d]	—	—	—	569	1	25
Suburban high schools[e]	—	—	—	516	5	51
Normal school[f]	—	—	—	69	1	8

Table 1 (*cont.*)

	1850			1876		
	Enroll-ment	No. of Schools	No. of Teachers	Enroll-ment	No. of Schools	No. of Teachers
School for deaf mutes[g]	—	—	—	1		8
School for licensed minors[h]	—	—	—	1		2
Kindergarten[i]	—	—	—	1		1
Evening schools[j]	—	—	—	17		142
Evening drawing schools[k]	—	—	—	4		16
Totals		185	339		197	1,294

[a] Approximate figure.
[b] Established in 1635, took students of grammar as well as high school age.
[c] Established in 1821.
[d] Separated from normal school and established in 1872.
[e] Includes Brighton High School, established in 1841; Charlestown High School, 1848; West Roxbury High School, 1849; Roxbury High School, 1852; Dorchester High School, 1852. All came into Boston system as a result of annexation of respective towns.
[f] Established in 1852.
[g] Established in 1869.
[h] Established in 1867. A licensed minor was a newsboy.
[i] Established in 1870.
[j] Evening schools established in 1857, and evening high school in 1869.
[k] Established in 1870.
Note: Figures mask an internal change: Primary schools were not only consolidated and made larger but also graded, starting in 1857. Grading of grammar schools began in 1847.

D. Special Instructors[a]

1850	1876	
None	General supervisor of music	1
	Director of music	6
	Normal art instructor and general supervisor of drawing	1
	Special instructor in drawing	6
	Vocal and physical culture, high school	1
	Military drill, high school	1
	French, high school	5
	German, high school	3
	Sewing, grammar school[b]	26
	Truant officers	14

[a] Special instructors are also included in numbers of teachers in part C.
[b] Authorization to teach sewing given in 1854.

Table 1 (*cont.*)

E. School Expenditures

	1850	1876
Total	$311,494.95	$15,252,199.73
Per pupil	$10.65	$29.88
Tax rate[a]	.00092	.00186

[a] Amount per dollar of assessed valuation raised by taxes for school support.

F. Population

	1850	1876
Total	138,788	341,919
Ages 5–15	24,275	66,720

Table 2

Hierarchy of Teaching Positions and Salaries

	1850	1876
High school teachers, male	Ranks: master, submaster Latin school, submaster English school, usher	Termed first-grade teachers. Ranks: headmaster, master, submaster, usher
	Salary range: $800–2,400 ($1,320–3,750)[a]	Salary range: $1,700–4,000, including increments within each position
High school teachers, female	None	Termed third-grade teachers. Ranks: assistant principal; first, second, third, and fourth assistants; normal-school assistant
		Salary range: $1,000–2,000
Grammar school teachers, male	Ranks: grammar and writing, master, usher	Termed second-grade teachers. Ranks: masters, submasters, ushers
	Salary range: $300–1,500 ($490–2,960)	Salary range: $1,700–3,200, including increments within each position
Grammar school teachers, female	(Salary of grammar school teachers not differentiated by sex; most likely all those labeled assistant were female)	Termed fourth-grade teachers. Ranks: first, second, and third assistants

Table 2 (*cont.*)

	1850	1876
		Salary range: $600–1,200, with increments only for third assistants
Primary school teachers	Primary school teacher	Termed fifth-grade teachers. Rank: fourth assistant
	Salary: $300 ($490)	Salary range: $600–800
Special teachers	None	Termed special grade teachers. 36 different positions, e.g., director of drawing, music
		Top salary: $3,300
Supervisory personnel	None	Three types: superintendent, $4,500; supervisor, $4,000; principal, paid according to teaching rank held.

a Figures in parentheses indicate approximate value of 1850 salaries adjusted for changes in cost of living to 1876 equivalents.

ond element in Friedrich's definition, was also apparent in both ways he has used the term. First, technical differentiation occurred as administrative duties became fixed and defined by regulation and as departments, specialist teachers, specialized schools, and age-grading were introduced. The practice of requiring all teachers to teach all subjects altered with the emergence of a whole corps of specialist instructors, most of whom traveled between two or more schools, teaching only their specialty. The second sort of differentiation, the development of hierarchy, emerged as the number of ranks within the system expanded and the salary gap between the highest and lowest positions widened.

The third element of bureaucracy is "qualification for office"—that is, appointment and promotion on the basis of objective qualifications. In 1850 the loose rules for the examination of teachers were applied casually, and the examinations themselves were conducted by amateurs whose capacity for determining the fitness of a candidate for teaching was undetermined. The teachers themselves, by and large, had had no specific pedagogical training. By 1876 the level of appointment of a teacher supposedly rested on predetermined, professionally derived and administered standards; examinations, now much more formal, were conducted by the supervisors, and which of the different classes of certificates was awarded to the candidates depended on their performance on the tests. A sizable proportion of teachers, moreover, now had been trained in normal schools, especially the one operated by the city.

The Boston school system for the most part reflected the behavioral as well as the organizational elements of bureaucracy. One such behavioral element is "objectivity" or "expertise" in performance. Innovations and administrative decisions had traditionally been made by amateur lay officials without professional advice or opinions. By 1876 an increasing number of decisions were being left to the career administrators, and, with some notable exceptions, the career administrators (considered "experts") exerted more and more influence on the decisions of the school board itself.

"Precision and continuity" constitute a second behavioral aspect of bureaucracy. Only meager statistics were gathered in 1850; there was no set pattern for administrative routine; the whims and preferences of lay officials largely governed their administrative and supervisory actions, which consequently had little consistency. By 1876 the gathering of elaborate statistics to serve as a basis for analysis and decision-making had become an established custom; rules existed to routinize administrative decisions and introduce consistency. In one respect, however, the Boston school system did not reflect this element of bureaucracy, for, despite the complaints of schoolmen and their supporters, there was no tenure system to assure continuity of personnel, and both administrators and teachers remained quite insecure.

The final element of bureaucratic behavior is "discretion."

No secret or private information was gathered in Boston in 1850; in 1876, however, the supervisors introduced a "black book," in which they recorded judgments on individual teachers. The book, which became infamous among the teachers, was open only to the school board and superintendent.

The bureaucratization of the Boston school system between 1850 and 1876 illustrated a general process taking place in other aspects of American urban life. In Boston, for instance, the various functions originally associated with the police were gradually being assigned to new, specialized agencies, and the police force itself was becoming professionalized and more elaborate in organization. The bureaucratization of urban education elsewhere was made clear by commentators who tried to describe American education in the 1870's and 1880's. Take, as an example, the critical description by Burke A. Hinsdale, then President of Hiram College in Ohio:

Our common schools constitute a highly complex and differentiated, a vast and powerful system. The machinery of this system is tens of thousands of school houses, thousands of libraries, vast illustrative apparatus, boards of directors and boards of examiners, normal schools and institutes, reports and bureaus, commissioners and superintendents, and more than a quarter of a million of teachers. In the towns and cities, the system has taken on a form especially complex and costly. There are the primary, grammar and high schools, with their grades, A, B, C, and D, not to mention the minor divisions which a layman can hardly keep in his head while hearing them; each one of which divisions is supposed to represent some definable stage in the training of a man. There are the teachers of the various grades, from the primary teachers up by way of the principal to the Superintendent of Public Instruction and his staff of assistants. Behind these come trooping in the kindergarten teachers, the normal and training teachers, followed by the music and drawing masters—each one having his bundle of reports under his arm and his sheet of percentages in his hand. The whole body of public school teachers constitute an intelligent, active and powerful profession; presenting in some respects the appearance of an hierarchy of education.

To describe the creation of bureaucracy in Boston or elsewhere, important as that task is, is not to explain why urban school systems became bureaucracies in the third quarter of the nineteenth century. From the timing of the various developments in Boston, one important fact about the nature of bureaucratization becomes clear: It did not emerge full blown. Although the structural features of the Boston school system were clearly interrelated, they had developed singly and at different times. In this sense "bureaucratization" can be a somewhat misleading term, unless one realizes that it is being used to encompass a number of distinct innovations and alterations, such as age-grading, the introduction of a superintendent, and the centralization of the school board. Bureaucratization, that is, was a piecemeal process. Thus, an account of the reasons for each structural change is necessary in order to explain the development of bureaucracy. However, a more general approach to the problem is still possible, because underlying the different innovations were certain pressures and predicaments that forced educational development in the direction of bureaucracy.

Perhaps the most fundamental problem facing school systems was the increasing complexity of the task of administering urban education. For example, in 1855 the city of Boston had only a superintendent and a school committee of seventy-six part-time lay members to supervise and coordinate more than 160 primary schools, which fed nearly fifty grammar schools that led, in turn, to the two high schools. As a part-time pursuit of busy people, the school committee could not oversee the work of individual schools with any care. Under the recently abolished primary school committee, at least someone had been responsible for each school. In some cases this undoubtedly led to close if paternalistic supervision. Now, however, the schools, taught by largely untrained young girls chosen by haphazard methods, were left without guidance. The superintendent, for all his remarkable energy, certainly could not regularly visit and advise more than 200 schools. Thus, there was little coordination or direction in the school system, which was staggering under an increasingly crowded and heterogeneous population. Grammar school masters had no assurance that the children coming to them from the primary schools had received a reasonably systematic, competently taught primary education. Nor, on the other hand, could the high schools be certain that their students had a reasonably common educational background. No reliable or systematic process existed for weeding out ineffectual teachers or for preventing their entry into the system at the primary level. In short, it was argued, to function with any degree of efficiency and effectiveness the school system desperately needed some coordination and increased supervision. In 1851 that line of argument had been effective in persuading the school committee to hire the first superintendent; it was convincing in 1876 in spurring the appointment of a board of supervisors and in streamlining the school committee. The argument was effective, too, in making the grammar school masters principals of the primary schools in their districts.

The complexity of administration was an implicit assumption in the educational ideal of urban superintendents throughout the country, who argued that all large organizations, from industry to the army, depended for coordination on centralized professional direction by a superintending officer. The success of professional supervision, especially in the various branches of industry, indicated the need for the same type of direction in education. Supervision was deemed necessary because organizations had to be based on division of labor, which, to these superintendents, was the process underlying social development. According to the influential superintendent and professor of pedagogy William H. Payne, the growth of civilization represented "a process of differentiation," whose stages of progress could be measured by the degree of functional separation between activities. Differentiation within school systems was thus an integral and progressive part of the development of a more civilized and complex society. And this differentiation introduced a need for specialization and coordination not present in earlier periods. Underlying the belief in the necessity of division of labor in school management was the assumption that the growing size and expanded role of the schools had made their management a far more difficult and specialized task than it had been. Thus, schoolmen saw such innovations as the superintendency, the elaboration of hierarchy, and specialization as necessary ways of meeting their increasingly complex tasks.

Schoolmen over and over again used the example of industry as an idealized standard that formed the basis for their justifications of the superintendency. They often described their school systems as factories and used metaphors based on the corporation and the machine. Modern industry, they could see, had developed its remarkable capacity through a rational organization that stressed hierarchy, the division of labor, and intensive professional supervision. If those methods worked in industries as diverse as textiles and railroads, why would they not work in education? Still, it is unlikely that schoolmen attempted to model their systems directly on factories. They never advocated so minute a division of labor, for instance, nor did they ask for quite so much passivity in their teachers, as supervisers of factories required of their workers. An intensive comparative analysis of school and factory organization in the period has yet to be made, but it is likely that such an analysis would find that schoolmen used the industrial analogy loosely, to justify the introduction and elaboration of certain general features of their school systems, such as supervision and departmentalization. This supposition is reinforced by the very vagueness with which industrial analogies were employed. No superintendent made a close study of the structure of industry or bothered to discriminate between service and production industries. Nor did any of them see any inconsistency in switching from an industrial analogy to a military one. Rather, the success of industry highlighted the relevance to schools of certain general features of organizations because both factory and school superintendent were faced with the same underlying problem: the coordination of large numbers of people in a complex enterprise, Because industry had seemingly conquered the problem of coordination, it offered valuable lessons for public education.

Schoolmen pointed out that a professionally supervised school system based on the division of labor should ideally have certain structural features and that its participants should have certain attitudes. An elaborate hierarchical structure and an explicit chain of command were necessary to keep each member working at his particular task in a responsible and coordinated fashion. At the head of the hierarchy should be one "vested with sufficient authority" to "devise plans in general and in detail" and to "keep all subordinates in their proper places and at their assigned tasks." Within the hierarchy, moreover, roles and duties should be defined clearly to avoid the possibility of conflict, and all members should give unquestioning, prompt obedience to the orders of their superiors. The great danger in a complex organization, according to Payne, was "disintegration," caused chiefly by "nonconformity," something not to be tolerated in either pupils or teachers.

To perfect their hierarchies, schoolmen argued, it was necessary to carry the development of career lines within school systems even further. If education was to become an attractive profession to men, "promotion from the ranks" was an absolute requisite. The introduction of tenure and pensions was also needed, they asserted. Subject to annual election by a school board, superintendents and teachers were thoroughly insecure and forced into timidity for the sake of survival. Moreover, the teacher, generally paid a meager salary, was unable to save and had to teach until he was forced from the classroom by total disability or death. When all teachers were offered a career, security, and protection from arbitrary dismissal, schoolmen asserted, hierarchical systems would be nearly perfect.

Bureaucratic innovations were introduced as part of a continuing process of rationalizing and coordinating the increasingly complex urban school systems. Added to the challenge of complexity were the problems of politics and personalities. Hardly anyone at the time would have quarreled with the position that teachers should be chosen for their qualifications and not for reasons of personal favoritism or nepotism. But diffuse, lay-controlled school systems made objectivity a scarce commodity. Politics exacerbated the situation, for to anchor school boards to city wards was to put them in the midst of the most intense political pressures, with often predictable results. Features of bureaucracy designed to provide impartial standards and centralize control were defenses against favoritism. The introduction of supervisors in Boston, for instance, was considered a means of lifting the appointment of teachers above the personal, amateur, and political level, since the supervisors conducted examinations for training positions. The development of more elaborate and specific written regulations was intended to make the operation of the school system more routine—that is, more impartial and equitable—and the removal of the school board from ward politics was designed to remove the schools from partisanship as well as to foster increased coordination through centralization.

Another reason for the development of bureaucracy is critical: It offered specific advantages to practicing schoolmen in their quest for "professionalism." It therefore enlisted their wholehearted and vigorous support. The first of these advantages we have already noted: the development of career lines within education. Superintendents fostering the elaboration of hierarchies were really creating careers for themselves and their contemporaries. Partly, their motivation was undoubtedly altruistic: a desire to create conditions that would attract more able men into education. Partly, too, they no doubt wished to improve their own chances of advancement; those who had reached top positions could see in hierarchy an augmenting of their own power, as armies of subordinates became increasingly subject to their control.

Bureaucratization also served schoolmen by mitigating an emerging problem: the regulation of behavior within the occupation itself. The concern of schoolmen with this issue was disclosed by Thomas Bicknell, in a presidential address to the National Council of Education. Bicknell noted that the alluring prospect of a rapidly ascending career was tempting ambitious individuals and often introducing into school systems destructive careerist competition that generated hostility and tension among an entire staff. The division of educational opinion in the country offered "perpetual temptation" to "undignified intrigue" and "violent excitement." The newly formed Council, composed of the elite of practicing American educators, would serve as a "warning to ambitious young teachers" by offering authoritative pronouncements on the bewildering array of innovations being peddled around the country. Most likely, schoolmen hoped that the Council would reinforce on a national level the sort of regulation of behavior that bureaucracies were trying to enforce on a local level. Bureaucracy places a premium on acquiescent, rule-following behavior. In this type of organization the individualist, the aggressively ambitious, is not only uncomfortable but unacceptable. The instruments that educational bureaucrats had for regulating behavior were uniform rules and prescribed patterns of action (such as centrally defined courses of study), coupled with the sanctions of colleagueship and promotion obtainable only for faithful service and quiet good behavior.

Schoolmen undoubtedly hoped to reduce the tension and the threat to themselves that arose from eccentric and innovative behavior on the part of such mavericks as the superintendent of Quincy, Mass., Francis Parker.

Thus, in the third quarter of the nineteenth century, increasingly complex administrative problems, reinforced by the nepotism and politics that afflicted school practice, made rationalization and coordination a necessity for urban school systems. Faced with this need, schoolmen (and some laymen as well) justified their organizing principles by analogies from industry, which they believed had successfully solved the same basic problem: the management of large numbers of people performing different tasks. The process of bureaucratization within education was so thorough and so rapid because of the enthusiasm of the schoolmen themselves, who saw in the new organizational forms the opening up of careers and a partial solution to the problem of regulating behavior within the occupation.

The schoolmen's ability to foster the development of hierarchical differentiated systems as rapidly as they did was due to another important factor: They met little opposition. One reason was that in the beginning influential laymen agreed with their goals. Bureaucracy, as we have observed, represented a crystallization of bourgeois social values. Besides, particular innovations in the direction of bureaucracy often gave differential advantage to the children of the affluent. Complementing that fact, the years of the rapid spread of bureaucracy were precisely the years of withdrawal of lay interest in education. By the mid-1850's, the first enthusiastic phase of the ante bellum educational revival had begun to decline, and the lay interest that had sustained the movement dwindled. The ante bellum reformers, however, had planted the seeds of bureaucracy by fostering an increase in the number of common schools and teachers, by urging grading, and by sponsoring the development of high schools. They had, moreover, called into being the first professional administrators, the superintendents, to help them with the management of these rather sprawling and uncoordinated systems. As lay interest lessened, the new class of professional educators consolidated the systems they had inherited. For roughly two decades, schoolmen were able to carry on the task of consolidation with a minimum of lay interference. In the process they introduced into the new school systems the features of bureaucracy that I have been examining. The withdrawal of lay zeal had left school systems open to capture by the professionals, who, quickly perceiving the advantages of bureaucracy, had acted with dispatch to build large, hierarchical, differentiated, uniform, and rigid organizations.

Critics of Education: The New School Board vs. *John Dudley Philbrick*

In the 1870's, a wave of criticism of the public schools spread throughout the country. Critics aimed their attacks at the results of public education, at its bureaucratic structure, and, especially in the beginning, at its costs. As citizens around the country searched for means of trimming municipal expenses in the aftermath of the depression of 1873, they turned their attention to the schools with an intensity that generally had been lacking for nearly two decades, and they noted with alarm that expenditures for public education had mounted enormously since the 1850's. Indeed, although financing remained far from adequate, one of the successes of the new class of career administrators had been in persuading the public to spend steadily increasing amounts of money on their schools. When laymen turned to the schools with renewed attention in the hope of cutting costs, they discovered to their horror that the quality of education was dreadfully low and, so they said, had actually declined. By 1875 the sentiment of community leaders in Boston, reflecting national criticism of public education, clearly favored a radical reform in the school system. The editor of the *Transcript*, for one, observed that "grave doubts are creeping about as to the absolute perfection claimed and conceded for the school system. . . . The system is, first, too costly, and next, too vital if it cost nothing, to escape criticism much longer."

Aside from the desire to cut expenses, reformers, at the start of their campaign, would have found it hard to express their goals precisely. The concrete aims of the reformist movement emerged, as we shall see, in the course of its development. In the beginning, reformers seemed to feel that something was wrong with the schools: Children learned too little and that not well; the atmosphere of the schools was too rigid and mechanical; the key personnel of the system exerted too strong a hold on its operation. Fresh thinking was imperative.

The first actions of the would-be reformers were contradictory. Their initial achievement was to obtain from the state legislature a bill calling for the appointment of supervisors by the school board and reducing the board from 118 members elected from wards to 24 elected at large. On the one hand, this action represented an attempt to continue the trend toward centralization of power and increased expertise in administration, classic aspects of bureaucratization that had marked educational development in Boston for twenty-five years. But the reformers were also concerned to change the operation of the system itself and to break the hold of the existing leaders. Because they felt considerable contempt for the career personnel of the schools, they went about their attempt to improve the system in a way that deliberately undercut the authority of the superintendents by failing to define and demarcate clearly the duties and spheres of influence of the supervisors, the new addition to the hierarchy. Thus the reformers' actions contradicted their professed ideal of rational, centralized organization. The immediate result was an ambiguity of role definition for administrators within the system and, hence, a vicious conflict that effectively prevented the new administrative arrangements from doing much good.

Opponents of the measure pointed out that the motivation behind the legislation changing the nature of school administration appeared to be more complex than a simple effort to bring about reform through centralization. Most of the opposition came from Catholics who believed the maneuver was intended to exclude them from the management of school affairs. They asserted, too, that the bill had been pushed through the school committee in an illegal and clandestine manner. Of course, no supporters of the legislation ever openly admitted to any anti-Catholic sentiment, although that may well have been part of their motivation. They based their case, and it was a good one, on the inefficiency of a large board, the preponderance of unqualified members, and the danger that partisan politics and even corruption might enter school affairs conducted at the ward level.

Leading citizens in Boston, like their counterparts elsewhere, were searching for a way of overcoming the partisanship and corruption that had entered the political life of the expanding city. While the reorganization of the school committee was being proposed, the legislature was considering (and ultimately rejected) a new city charter designed to mitigate partisan politics in city affairs by increasing the power of intelligent and disinterested public executives. Parallel efforts were under way in other places. For instance, accompanying the introduction of the superintendency in the town of Quincy was a change in the method of the town meeting, designed to remove essential decisions from the mass of the participants; accompanying the reorganization of the school committee in Boston was an attempt to change the nature of city government; in both places, municipal and educational reforms were part of a program for overcoming the weaknesses of urban democracy. Here is where, in a modified form, the charges of the Catholics probably had some validity. Mugwumps like Charles Francis Adams, Jr., who sponsored the reform in Quincy, held the immigrants and their spokesmen responsible for a decline in the quality of municipal life; consequently, attempts to reform civic conduct were, by definition, efforts to reduce the power of the newcomers.

The first important task of the streamlined Boston school board was to elect a superintendent, for in the middle of 1874 John Dudley Philbrick, who had been superintendent since 1856, had resigned. Philbrick was an important man in educational circles that extended beyond Boston. The editor of the *New England Journal of Education* called him "a representative American educator," and the phrase was quite accurate. At one time or another, Philbrick was president of almost every important state and national educational association. He was far more than a local superintendent; he was one of the few recognized spokesmen for American schoolmen. One reason for Philbrick's resignation, offered in retrospect, was ill health, but it is likely that he sensed the impending change in school organization and wanted to give the new board a chance to start afresh with a new superintendent. That the new board might want a different superintendent he had good reason to believe, because the growing public dissatisfaction with the schools reflected more than a little on his management. Although the representative of the schoolmen's interests in Boston, the *New England Journal of Education,* expected that Philbrick would be chosen again, his candidacy ran into serious trouble as a faction of the school board, in a surprise move, tried to elect someone else to the superintendency. Philbrick was re-elected despite the opposition, but his position as superintendent, with a goodly portion of his aggressively reformist school board against him, was shaky, to say the least.

After choosing a superintendent, the board had to elect six people to fill the newly created, important, and highly paid ($4,000 a year) positions of supervisors. The duties of the supervisors were far from clear. The act that had established the school board merely stated that six supervisors should be appointed, leaving the definition of their duties to the board. Together with the superintendent as chairman, the six supervisors formed the board of supervisors; they were left virtually free to develop examinations and to organize the way in which they would carry out their other assignments.

Here it is critical to note that the line between the duties of the supervisors and those of the superintendent was far from clear. The school board had created an imperfect hierarchy whose top members had overlapping authority and duties, a situation bound to breed trouble. The potential for conflict was increased by the nature of the appointments themselves. A committee of the school board nominated twelve people as supervisors, of whom the first six in order of preference were practicing schoolmen. Had those six been elected, much of the trouble that ensued would have been avoided, for they and Philbrick would have shared common assumptions about their respective duties and authority and about the management of urban schools.

The reform faction within both school board and city was not satisfied; when the balloting was over, only two of the committee's first choices had been elected. The remaining four new supervisors were men with little practical experience in public education. The majority of the supervisors, in short, represented the lay reformist interest on the school board. The result of the school board's inconsistency was predictable: By electing both Philbrick, a schoolman of known views and temperament, and a majority of supervisors representing lay reformist interests, people whose views would conflict with his, the board set the stage for the debilitating quarrel that rocked Boston's schools during the next eight years.

Throughout the first year under the new arrangement, the conflict between the board of supervisors and the superintendent simmered just barely below the surface. By the end of the year it had come into full public view. It was, of course, not only Philbrick who looked with some suspicion at the new board; the grammar and high school masters liked it no better. The teachers knew of the secrecy involved in the supervisors' operations; they were rated by the "supervisors according to a numerical scale in a book open not for our inspection but to the inspection of the committee." They realized that their "work was reported on and . . . defects noted in another book, also open to the committee but not to us." Therefore, the teachers regarded supervision as a "euphemistic term for espionage. There was a widespread prejudice against it. Although hostile to the supervisors, the teachers did not complain publicly, for their position was painfully tenuous. Each year they faced re-election by the school board, and public criticism of school policy could easily cost an experienced teacher his job. Complained one commentator, "It is a notorious fact that the mouths of our teachers are closed."

Philbrick acted with surprising force to discredit the work of the supervisors. In a section of his semiannual report entitled "The New Departure," he attacked the plan of work adopted by the supervisors. So incensed was the school board by his action that it forced him to expurgate the report. Although the officially published document did not contain Philbrick's accusations, he nevertheless published the original version of his report separately and reprinted the offending section in the *New England Journal of Education*.

The school board itself moved more and more toward the side of the supervisors. Because of the intense and now public controversy, two subcommittees were appointed to investigate the relationship between superintendent and supervisors. The first offered, in vague language, an unconvincing elaboration of the supervisors' point of view and an exoneration of the regulations governing their actions. The second, instead of offering substantive motions, tried to analyze the source of the friction; its only contribution was the pious hope that the two sides could settle their differences peacefully. Philbrick himself showed a desire to moderate the conflict. For some time he had held monthly meetings of the grammar and high school masters, and at one of these in 1876 he had described the reasons for the reorganization of the school committee and asked the masters for cooperation.

Philbrick's attempt to reach a compromise with the supervisors failed. As the reformist influence on the school board grew more dominant, his position progressively worsened. By January, 1878, the time for the next election of a superintendent, his fate was clear. After twenty-two years of hard service as superintendent of schools, Philbrick was unceremoniously fired. In any event such a situation would not lack pathos, but the harshness of the act was underscored by Philbrick's "expressed desire to be vindicated by a re-election, after which he was determined to resign." Ruthlessly bent on change, the school board would not allow Philbrick the dignity of an honorable retirement.

It is hard not to sympathize with Philbrick in his quarrel with the school board. He had labored long and energetically to construct and operate a school system. He had worked without any security in a city subject to all the stresses and frustrations that accompanied late-nineteenth-century population growth and urban politics. In this trying setting he had managed not only to hang onto his job, a feat not to be taken lightly, but also to bring increasing order and system to the schools of Boston. True, he ran an expensive school system, but his plausible answer to this criticism was, first, that fewer children attended private and parochial schools in Boston than in any other large city and, second, that good schools were expensive. That the schools were good by the standards of the time is a conclusion reinforced by the reports of many foreign observers who claimed that the Boston schools were the best in the nation. But the issue was not a simple one, and virtue did not reside entirely on Philbrick's side. Philbrick

lacked imagination, vision, and the desire or instinct to innovate radically. His ideal of education was dull, mechanical,
and rigid. It is unclear just what further progress education in
Boston would have made under his continued direction, aside
from a further systematization of administration, and it is unlikely that he would have inspired the reforms in pedagogy
and tone necessary to infuse vitality into the classrooms. Insofar as the reformers had as their goal the kind of freeing of the
curriculum and change in spirit that Francis Parker effected in
nearby Quincy, they were urging innovations that were needed
by urban schools. And their perception that the existing key
people in the Boston schools, the superintendent and his lieu-
tenants, the grammar masters, would not introduce those
reforms without a hard shove from an outside source was
undoubtedly accurate. But the reformers lacked sensitivity
and a sense of strategy. They had no realistic idea of how to
effect the changes they desired, and they were totally unaware
and careless of the feelings of those they would reform, so cal-
lous that they could fire John Dudley Philbrick a few months
before he intended to retire.

The school board undoubtedly hoped that Philbrick was
sufficiently crushed to sink quietly into oblivion. But he was
not to be silenced, and he added to the bitterness aroused by
his firing by sending a long defensive letter to the *Transcript*.
Nor did the school board count on the possibility that Philbrick might rise to even greater eminence and thereby attain
a position from which he could counterattack with increased
prestige and authority. But that is what happened, for in
March, 1878, Philbrick left the superintendency of the Boston
schools to become United States Commissioner of Education
at the Paris Exposition. Temporarily he was gone from Boston, but, if the school committee breathed a sigh of relief, it
was a sigh of false optimism. The submerged anger of the
masters at Philbrick's firing made further trouble inevitable.
Philbrick, as I have noted, had promoted the interests of the

masters and increased their powers substantially. In turn he had won their loyalty. The school board had seriously underestimated both the popularity and the strength of their opponent and the resistance of his supporters. By firing Philbrick it had not quieted but instead inflamed the controversy.

The removal of Philbrick ended the first phase of the dispute, which had disclosed one of the problems inherent in the development of a bureaucracy—namely, the definition of roles. When bureaucracy arises in piecemeal fashion, as it did in Boston, the demarcation of duties and lines of authority becomes blurred, and tensions arising from overlapping functions are almost inevitable. In Boston this problem was exacerbated by the sloppy way in which the school board went about the process of organization-building. The board members in those years proved to be both bad bureaucrats and ineffectual reformers. Instead of rejuvenating the schools, all they did was cause trouble. Although they may have had a more lively idea of the possibilities of education than Philbrick did, they did not share his understanding of organizations and their constraints. After it had disposed of Philbrick, the reformist faction attempted to go about its job in a more thorough, ruthless, and efficient manner. But, again, it ultimately failed because of its insensitivity to the nature of organization. In this case, the aspect of organization the reformers failed to reckon with was the power of entrenched informal groups within the system itself.

Critics of Bureaucracy: The Attack on the Grammar School Masters

The Boston school board added to its problems by its choice of a successor to Philbrick. Samuel Eliot (a relative of Harvard's president) had little practical experience in the administration of public education. Following his graduation from Harvard (first in his class), Eliot had toured Europe and written a series of history books. In 1856, aged 35, Eliot became Professor of History and Political Science at Trinity College, Hartford, and from 1860 to 1866 he served as Trinity's president. In 1874 (the intervening eight years are vague) he became principal of the Girls' High and Normal School in Boston but resigned the position after only two years because of ill health and family bereavement. The scholarly Eliot, near-amateur in public school affairs, appealed to the reformist element of the school board, and his reports quickly made it evident that he sympathized with the faction that had deposed Philbrick. Eliot's snobbish social Darwinism and isolation from the schools compounded his problems. As a practical administrator, he was generally inept. In contrast to Philbrick's reports, Eliot's were filled not with pragmatic discussions of practical subjects but with long and florid discourses more suited to a late-nineteenth-century literary magazine than to the reports of an urban superintendent.

Throughout 1878 the reformist faction continued to gain power. At the annual election later in the year, fourteen of the twenty-four places on the school committee passed to new people. Although one new member, former grammar school master George Hyde, was a solid schoolman, the new committee, led by Brooks Adams, was heavily reformist in composition. Adams had a model for educational reform in the experience of his older brother, Charles Francis Adams, Jr., who had been deeply involved in the school reform of nearby Quincy, the movement usually associated with Francis Parker.

Ebullient, charismatic, and a thoroughgoing individualist, Parker was described by one influential school observer as the "poet of the new elementary education." Upon his return from studying educational theory and practice in Europe, he had so captivated the school board of Quincy (including Charles Francis Adams, Jr., that they had given him virtually complete control of school policy, with the exception of finances, and a mandate to revolutionize the town's schools. Parker justified their expectations by radically altering the curriculum, pedagogy, and tone of the Quincy schools. Through his own infectious zeal and love of children he had inspired the town's teachers to make their schools places where children's happiness was of paramount concern. Many of the thousands of observers who annually trooped to Quincy to view Parker's work, loudly advertised by the Adamses and other school board members, testified to his success. And it was not only the tone of the school that he changed. A comparative analysis of educational achievement in Quincy and elsewhere showed that, where Parker's influence had been strongest, children had actually learned to read, write, and cipher much better. At the same time Parker managed to double the enrollment of the high school, eliminate the problem of irregular attendance, and almost end truancy, feats that other Massachusetts towns and cities had been striving unsuccessfully to achieve for decades.

Boston's new school board, like Quincy's, offered a diagnosis of educational ills that reflected the concern of lay reformers throughout the country about the cost and quality of education. Added to this was their often subtle perception of the consequences of bureaucratic rigidity, in particular the effects of bureaucracy on the personalities and behavior of its members. "Many minds," wrote one critic, "are incapable of using forms without becoming their slaves." Equally unfortunate was the fact that routine and ritual drive a wedge between teacher and pupil, altering what had once been a much more vital and meaningful relationship. The "personal force of the teacher," Burke Hinsdale lamented, "goes for much less," and the pupil receives far less "inspiration" than before. The old "no-system" plan was, he felt, far more conducive "to developing individuality of character." In the process of becoming slaves to the routine of formal requirements, teachers lost their perspective and acquired "a tendency . . . to exaggerate little things—to sink the important." One effect of bureaucracy on behavior was to turn means into ends. All of the pressures on the teachers reinforced that effect. The city schoolman, by an "acquired bias of mind," had become a "martinet" who liked "the machine better the stiffer and firmer it can be made." By stressing the meek acceptance of orders from superiors, the system "narrows responsibility and stifles thought"; it thus becomes "death to all inventive minds."

The more perceptive critics, like Hinsdale and Charles Francis Adams, Jr., saw the dilemma that faced would-be educational reformers. Hinsdale was too shrewd and realistic to believe that anyone could reverse the direction of development and return to the old no-system plan of public education, even if it had in its day produced better results. Organization was necessary. Still, organization stamped out spontaneity and originality. Here was the dilemma, and to his credit Hinsdale recognized it in all its complexity. "You cannot have the greatest personal intrepidity and the best organization—the most individuality of character and the best organization—the most individuality of character and the most imposing array of school children and schoolmasters." "How," he asked, looking for a compromise, "shall we combine both elements most wisely?"

For all his perceptiveness, Hinsdale had little to offer in reply to his question; his only concrete suggestion was to prune and steamline the curriculum, which had become burdened with so many subjects that teachers, just to cover the ground, were forced into mechanical presentations. But that solution touched only the packed curriculum, which made rigid, crowded timetables a necessity; it did not provide ways of lessening the effects of a centralized, hierarchical structure on the teachers and pupils. In short, it missed the underlying dimensions of the problem and offered only a partial solution to the tough and troubling question Hinsdale had asked. No one else, unfortunately, had a viable alternative to bureaucracy.

On the surface, the most promising alternative was offered by Charles Francis Adams, Jr., but this, too, had serious deficiencies. More than any other critic, Adams accepted the need for a planned hierarchical educational structure. His goal was to reduce the mechanical, formalistic tone of the structure by infusing it with new vigor and life. To accomplish this he proposed a revitalized superintending class trained "scientifically" in universities.

The weakness of that prescription was that Adams was generalizing from his experience with a seemingly successful educational reform movement in Quincy, a town of only 10,000 people. He assumed that one intelligent man of magnetic personality, trained in educational science, could single-handedly rejuvenate an entire bureaucratic school system, as Francis Parker had done in Quincy, refining the necessary formal elements of that organization and simultaneously removing the deadening effect of systematizing upon its spirit. Adams perceived the influence that the structure of an organization could exert upon the temper of its operations and the personality of its participants, but he did not consider these effects inevitable and predicted that a single inspired leader could remove them. In a town of 10,000, charismatic bureaucracy might work for a time, as Francis Parker had proved. But in a city of hundreds of thousands, charismatic bureaucracy was a very insubstantial model on which to place one's hopes for a school system. Highly structured, hierarchical organizations are far harder to change than Adams thought, as was demonstrated in Boston by the experience of both Adams's brother Brooks (who obviously had been impressed with this model) and, later on, by Francis Parker.

In Boston the reformers, who agreed with the analyses of the critics of educational bureaucracy, assumed that they could draw up a new blueprint for the city's schools and simply put it into effect. They realized that some resistance would come from teachers, especially grammar school masters, but they reasoned, incorrectly, that they could easily break the masters' hold on the system by installing the supervisors, who they hoped would prove to be charismatic bureaucrats, in the place of the masters. Through executive fiat, they expected, the conduct of an entire school system and all the relations within it could be successfully altered.

On January 28, 1879, the new school board revealed its reformist aspirations when it appointed a committee on the revision of the school system. Between January and May, the committee, pursuing the twin objectives of economizing and improving, scrutinized virtually every facet of the school system and, in a series of six reports, offered recommendations for sweeping changes. The leading spirit of the revision committee and the author of its reports was generally acknowledged to be Brooks Adams.

Some of the revision committee's many recommendations were designed, despite superfluous rationalizations, merely to save money. Among them were the proposals to abolish the kindergarten and the intermediate schools and to reorganize and centralize the high school system, the new scheme for furnishing supplies to students, and the elimination of special instructors. Others were intended to have a more direct educational effect. They included the pruning of the curriculum (as recommended by Hinsdale), the adoption of the newly designed grammar school course, and the upgrading of the normal school by raising admission standards, adding a postgraduate year, and increasing the amount of practice teaching. By the end of the year, one goal seemed clearly in sight; the board reported with pleasure that it had already reduced per-pupil spending in Boston, the highest in the nation, and expected the decrease to continue.

The most controversial and consequential recommendation

of the revision committee called for ending the supervision of the primary schools by the grammar school masters. Although this plan had once been necessary, it had never been entirely satisfactory in practice, argued the committee, because it made the masters both supervisors and teachers. To perform one duty well, they had to neglect the other; improvement in the primary schools was obtained at the expense of the grammar schools. Moreover, the masters diluted their influence by spreading it over a number of schools. For educational success, the committee was saying, personal appeal was as important as system, and it was this that the principalship of the masters had sacrificed.

As the committee analyzed the grammar school masters themselves, its real concerns began to emerge. Like lay reformers throughout the country, the committee believed that rigidity and formalism had stultified urban education, and reform required the exchange of mechanistic models and procedures for ones infused with vitality and enthusiasm. The results of the masters' principalship had been improvement, but it had been purchased with a needless circumscription of the "independence and individuality . . . of the subordinate instructors."

The reason lay in the effects of a hierarchical structure on personality, something the reformers in Boston realized quite as clearly as their counterparts around the country. Here the committee bared the part of its critique most galling to the masters and most certain to alienate those influential members of their school system. "The school-master," they wrote, "is proverbially dogmatic in his own sphere. . . . One tendency of his calling is to make him arbitrary." The supervision of the principals had been "overdone; and a check upon the tendency to 'machine school-keeping' [was required] not in the Primary Schools only, but also in the Grammar Schools."

To see how well the proposed new system would work, the

school board at the end of March placed one primary school under the care of a supervisor. Pleased with the results, the board decided to extend the experiment to all primary schools and consequently designated three supervisors to take charge of those schools. Superintendent Samuel Eliot showed his colors when he welcomed the change in primary school supervision and predicted its success in typically florid style. The school board and its new superintendent considered that education in Boston had become dry, rigid, and mechanistic, and the people who had permitted it to calcify were Philbrick, the man who had been superintendent for twenty-two years, and his loyal supporters, the grammar school masters. Reform required not only new curricula and more charismatic personnel but also a massive redistribution of power and influence. To effect such redistribution was the purpose of the removal of the grammar masters from the primary schools; to resist and sabotage this redistribution became the goal of the grammar school masters and their supporters.

Caught up in its desire to free the primary schools, the revision committee had neglected to consider the real unity and strength of the grammar school masters, whose close association and mutuality of interests had welded them into an influential informal organization (represented by the Boston Masters' Association) within the larger school system. For years, the masters had been meeting monthly for dinner and discussion of educational problems. Thus held together, the masters were in an effective position to undermine any educational reform they felt was unwise or threatening. By granting primary principalships, Philbrick had vastly increased the authority and power of the grammar school masters, making each of them, in a way, "a little king" in his district, and had thereby revealed his own shrewd sense of the conditions that create loyalty within a large organization.

Between Philbrick and the masters mutual loyalty and respect had developed, which reinforced the cohesiveness of the career schoolmen in the Boston system. Loyal to Philbrick, the masters had been enraged by his firing and were in no mood to cooperate with the board that had ousted him. In turn, when the masters were robbed of their power, Philbrick came to their defense with vigor. The sense of unity, the tight informal organization within the Boston school system, was something the reformers had been unable to perceive. Or, if they had perceived it, they were unable to realize that it was impossible to ride roughshod over such a group. They failed to understand that to introduce reforms they would have to have the masters on their side. Instead, the reformers (like their counterparts today) fomented a major battle, and in the end they lost.

The Defense of Bureaucracy: The Masters Counterattack

Opposition to the alteration in primary supervision arose quickly. After the publication of the first of the revision committee's reports in April, the *New England Journal of Education* violently attacked the proposed change. Afraid to speak out because of possible reprisals at the annual election, the masters published almost no criticism of the new arrangements, but their cause was championed by others, including the *Journal,* the prominent retired long-time Boston grammar master Joshua Bates, and, soon, Philbrick himself.

Philbrick, now newly distinguished, had returned from Paris early in 1880. Free of responsibility and the need to win re-election, he used his considerable influence to cause trouble for the school board and the supervisors. Philbrick bitterly resented the work of the revision committee, which destroyed many of the administrative features he had labored to introduce into the Boston school system. To Philbrick the committee's action represented a repudiation of his twenty-two years as superintendent, and he had no intention of receiving this insult in silence. He attended teachers' meetings, wrote letters to newspapers, meddled in the elections for the school board, and, most noticeably, between February and May, 1880, published a series of scathing articles in the *Journal of Education* reviewing the "new departure" in Boston. In these polemical articles Philbrick took apart, piece by piece, each of the changes instigated by the revision committee and, with much vehemence, the removal of the masters from the principalships of the primary schools.

Within the school board the masters had a few supporters, especially the retired master George Hyde. These men tried unsuccessfully to persuade the board to reverse its earlier decision and return the primary schools to the masters. At a school board meeting Hyde predicted (prophetically, as it turned out) "that within two years the primary schools would be under the charge of the masters, as they should be." The implication of impending counterattack in Hyde's remarks reflected an unofficial mobilization of professional forces in Boston and other cities as well.

Recall that schoolmen throughout the country were, like the Boston masters, under attack, and for many of the same reasons. The key men in the new urban school systems had to defend themselves against charges that they were contributing to a decline in the quality of public education by their rigid formalism, their exaltation of means over ends, their suppression of individuality, and their adoption of the personality and behavior of the drillmaster, revelling in the uniform, the petty, and the routine. To counter those serious accusations, educators in Boston and elsewhere developed a number of strategies. The opposition of the Boston grammar school masters and their supporters to the revision committee was one aspect of a larger counterattack against lay reformers across the country.

Representative of the attitude of schoolmen was the response of Cleveland's superintendent, ex-NEA president Andrew Rickoff, to Hinsdale's assertion that the quality of education had declined because of the development of highly differentiated, hierarchical, and uniform school systems. Rickoff's central argument was an open and unabashed defense of the type of educational system that had emerged in the cities. He insisted that graded schools, instead of hindering, helped the brightest pupils as well as the dullest by increasing the opportunities for individual attention. He extolled the reorganization of school systems on the principle of the division of labor, and he championed a centrally defined, rigid curriculum. By introducing plan and direction into education, a centrally planned syllabus spared the child from being buffeted back and forth between teachers with different ideas and approaches. "How," asked Rickoff, "shall unity of design in the fabric of education be guaranteed? We reply, in only one way, and that is by laying out our plans and specifications before the structure is commenced."

Rickoff's defense of a hierarchically structured, tightly organized, rigidly operated, centrally planned and directed school system made good sense in terms of efficiency. But, enmeshed in his school system as he had been for years, Rickoff was unable even to see what Hinsdale and other critics at their most perceptive had been deploring. Rickoff was unable, that is, to grasp the fact that Hinsdale and others had been lamenting the subtle effect of rigid structure on the temper of an institution and the personalities of its members. Because they were victims of this very effect, Rickoff and schoolmen who shared his views were simply unaware that there was any tension between originality and spontaneity, on the one hand, and efficiency in organization, on the other. For them there was no cost involved in building the increasingly characteristic administrative structure of urban education; bureaucratization was pure gain. It was, ironically, the inability of the schoolmen to appreciate the central point of the attacks that turned their defenses into sources of support for the accusations of their critics.

To defend bureaucracy on grounds of efficiency, harmony,

and rationality while ignoring its effects on the temper of the schools was a common strategy employed against critics of urban education. Another was to trim goals by bringing the objectives of public education into line with its actual achievements. Nowhere was this more evident than in the response of schoolmen to the accusations of Richard Grant White, the critic who aroused the most outrage and the most numerous counterattacks by arguing that the key assumption on which the case for public education had been advanced during the mid-century reform movement had been thoroughly disproved. The assumption, claimed White, was that public education was necessary to the social and moral life of a community: Education would bring about a decrease in crime, immorality, and other social ills. In part, White noted, the argument rested on a confusion of correlation with causation, because it assumed, from the frequent coexistence of ignorance and vice, that the former caused the latter. In reality, however, the two coexisted because they were both products of the same underlying problem: poverty. If the theory was true, White argued, then the tremendous investment in public education over several decades surely should have produced both a noticeable and measurable improvement in the quality of moral life and a decrease in crime. But everyone knew that the quality of life was steadily declining, that politics was ever more corrupt, that crime and vagrancy were on the increase. Despite massive attention to and expenditure on public education, asked White, "who needs to be told that in all these respects we have deteriorated?"

White damaged his clever case by using faulty statistics from the 1860 census, which, on the surface, seemed to show that Massachusetts, with a long tradition of public schools, had more crime, insanity, and suicide than Virginia, which, like most of the South, lagged in educational matters. But he was careful to insist that his argument not be taken to imply that education had caused the rise in crime and the decrease in morals. Rather, he emphasized, his point was simply that it had done nothing to stem these social maladies.

White's was one of the most damning and provocative indictments of public education America has seen, not so much for its denunciation of the lack of learning in the schools but for the way in which it hurled back the key assumptions of the school promoters. Although schoolmen had been arguing for decades that public schools would reform and uplift society both morally and economically, they too complained of the very social deficiencies that White lamented. If they admitted that society was still in a very bad way, then they were almost forced to accept the logic of White's ruthless argument, for public schools had been supported, maintained, and improved for a considerable period. Thus it followed clearly, in terms of the key arguments of the original mid-century promoters, that public schools had failed. The corollary was that the professional educators and planners of large, expensive school systems had likewise failed and were drawing their often sizable salaries on a fraudulent premise.

White's many attackers repeated the same points over and over again. One criticism was that his standing as an amateur made him incapable of judging the quality of education; another was that his attack revealed the antidemocratic animus that underlay most attacks on the schools; a third, and perhaps the most justified criticism was that his sources were faulty. But in all the rebuttals, White's professional critics refused to deal with his essential point that there was no essential relation between ignorance and crime, because both were products of poverty. In fact, most of them, including Philbrick, totally distorted the point in their attempts to discredit White, claiming, incorrectly, that White had asserted education caused crime.

Schoolmen explicitly and vigorously denied the accuracy of White's interpretation of the purpose of public education, although they did not generally state their version of the true theory. One reason they felt no need to offer proof that White was wrong was that in 1873 a group of prominent educators (including Philbrick), under the leadership of William Torrey Harris, had published a credo, widely taken as the official statement of the theory of education in the United States, and they considered reference to that statement sufficient to refute White's contentions about the social role of public schools both past and present. Any reading of earlier theorists like Horace Mann would show, they maintained, that public schools had never been viewed as social panaceas. Here White's critics were wrong, as Chapter 1 should have made clear. In contrast to Mann, the *Statement of Theory of Education* had a very different tone. It contained no passionate metaphors and no predictions that the school would conquer social ills; in sober, unemotional language, thoroughly unlike Mann's, it merely stated that *one* function of the school in America was "to train the pupil into habits of prompt obedience to his teachers and the practice of self-control in its various forms, in order that he may be prepared for a life wherein there is little police-restraint on the part of the constituted authorities." Although the tone of the later statement was less emotional, the idea that schools existed to promote law and order remained central to educational thought.

The sober and modest 1873 document, devoid of boastful or extravagant claims, is typical of the period. Parallels to Mann's emotional and optimistic rhetoric, quite common among those concerned with educational innovation and administration in the 1840's and 1850's, would be hard indeed to find in the 1870's and 1880's. The disagreement between White and his professional critics about the role of education is particularly significant because of the process it reveals. In the 1840's education promoters had labored to convert the people to the cause of public schools, which they evangelically described as prerequisites to a secular millennium. Their successors, the second generation of public school leaders, inherited the school systems that had been established by the mid-century innovators. As the new systems manifestly did not reach their original goals, the stated aims of education were gradually and quietly displaced by more limited and realistic expectations. This displacement was necessary because school administrators could no longer rely on the predictions of Horace Mann to justify the massive and expensive organizations they operated and expanded. The very survival of public education as a series of large bureaucratic school systems depended on the transformation of expectations. It was a real question, though, whether the survival of their organizations had become more important to schoolmen than the quality of education and the real needs of children.

Proclaiming the virtues of bureaucratic organizations, pointing out the enormous difficulties posed for the schools by their context, toning down the expectations for public education— these were the rhetorical strategies of defense used by career educators. In Boston and elsewhere definite activities were added, most notably the development of professional journals and organizations on a new scale. By the 1870's there existed a body of educators large enough and permanently and seriously enough concerned with schools to support national periodicals and to make regional and national organizations more viable.

The publications and organizations fostered, for one thing, a sense of community among administrators and teachers. In the pages of journals and at meetings, they had the satisfaction of sharing their problems and anxieties and knowing that they were by no means alone in their difficulties. The publications also gave them a forum in which to express criticism with relative safety. For instance, in its articles and editorial columns, the *New England Journal of Education* (as of 1881, when it became national, just *Journal of Education*) offered a strong and articulate defense of the career educators against lay critics, as well as a national platform from which to launch a counterattack. The editor, Thomas Bicknell, was in an ideal position to provide the schoolmen with support, for it was on *their* support, not on that of school boards or any other segment of the lay public, that the success of his journal depended. Bicknell thus could say what many others, circumscribed by insecure political situations, could only feel. It was through Bicknell, to take only one instance, that the Boston grammar school masters were able to mount their strong and ultimately successful counteroffensive against their critics. The potential that schoolmen saw in professional organization is illustrated clearly by the establishment in 1881 of the National Council of Education as a part of the NEA. Most fittingly, its first president was Bicknell. The council considered itself a forum for mediating the claims of the many new and conflicting ideas for educational innovation. Although it had no power of compulsion, the council hoped that stamping a particular point of view with its imprimatur would substantially influence educational practice, a critical consideration at that moment because of the combination of widespread acerbic criticism leveled at public education and serious disagreement on some important issues among educators themselves.

The experience of the Boston grammar school masters reinforced Bicknell's contentions, for their internal unity and lack of contention were precisely their source of strength. In Boston, opposition to reform took the form not only of protests by supporters of the masters but also of covert and hard-to-prove resistance by the masters themselves. As one commentator noted, the masters did not like the new arrangement and, "therefore, have tried . . . to ridicule the new system and throw obstacles in its way." It was widely believed, and probably with justification, that the masters were doing all they could to subvert the new supervisory arrangements. Without writing in the journals or otherwise opening themselves to demonstrable charges of insubordination, the masters used their strategic position, their combination of prestige, influence, and informal organization, their cohesiveness, to plan and execute tactics that would harass and destroy the "new departure."

The Triumph of Informal Organization: The Victory of the Masters

The hostility of the masters and the controversy within the system were too much for Samuel Eliot. The superintendent was unable—indeed, did not even try—to do anything to reduce the hostility between the reformist board and the masters. In fact, he had exacerbated the situation by taking the reformist side and alienating the masters. Unable to contain, much less resolve, the controversy, Eliot resigned in the middle of 1880, ostensibly because of ill health.

Apparently the attitude of the grammar school masters influenced the choice of the new superintendent, the principal of Boston English High School, Edwin Seaver, for he was a candidate welcomed by them and by the *New England Journal of Education*. Like Philbrick, Seaver quickly showed that he understood the need for the support of his teachers. At the first monthly meeting of the masters after his election, Seaver outlined "the motives which would govern his action." The editor of the *Journal* remarked slyly, "It was very fitting, too, that he should thank the teachers for the sympathy extended to him as well as for the congratulations." Seaver suggested to the masters that, when a policy they had criticized was adopted by the school board, "it would be the part of wisdom to 'let it run its race and be glorified,' or condemned." After the meeting Seaver "took his usual place at the monthly dinner of the masters, and that body . . . seemed indeed to justify the remark of one of the most eminent of their number, that they were 'very, very, happy again.'" With the appointment of Seaver and the consequent reunion of superintendent and masters, the strength in the controversy shifted markedly to the schoolmen. The denouement became simply a matter of time. But before the final actions had been taken, Boston passed through some more trials that revealed the inability of its bureaucracy to accommodate charismatic and individualistic personalities, for Francis Parker came to Boston, bringing with him one-fourth of Quincy's erstwhile teachers. It was not surprising that school reformers in Boston were eager to lure Parker to their city, and in 1881 the combination of a salary double the one he received in Quincy and the parsimoniousness of the Quincy school board, which made it unable to retain its best teachers, prompted Parker to accept the offer of a supervisorship in the Hub. "It is said," reported a very knowledgeable observer, that when Parker left Quincy he received this advice from Charles Francis Adams: "Get a new suit of clothes, a tall hat, and keep your mouth shut, if you wish to succeed." The advice was excellent, but Parker refused to heed at least the last part, and that contributed quite directly to his failure to work the revolution in Boston that he had in Quincy.

The appointment of Parker as a supervisor with special responsibility for Boston's primary schools revealed one goal of the reformist faction: the introduction of the Quincy system into the Boston primary schools. Most likely this objective had contributed to the school board's decision to remove the masters from the primary schools, for the masters were skeptical of the sort of innovation Parker represented. Stern traditionalists, they looked with skepticism on most of Parker's methods, especially the use of oral instruction, the relaxation of discipline, and the attempt to introduce "sunshine in the schoolroom."

Parker apparently decided that he would run his section of the city as he had run the schools of Quincy—personally and as he saw fit, with little reference to established procedures or even to the school board itself. He determined, so the story went, to prove the superiority of his system to all others by introducing it into the Prince School in Back Bay, where the rivalry from excellent prestigious private schools was keenest. Success gained in this school "would be relatively of greater importance than successes scored in two or three of our public schools elsewhere." To create his demonstration, Parker wanted to put a particular teacher from Quincy into the Prince School; his problem was that no vacancies existed there. So he decided to make one and executed a complex maneuver, described by his subsequent accusers as a game of checkers. The victim of Parker's game was Lydia A. Isbell, fourth assistant in the Blossom Street School. Mrs. Isbell, a widow who had grown up in the district of Boston in which she later taught, had served in the Blossom Street School for seventeen consecutive years. Her total service, in fact, had been nearly thirty years. After marriage she had moved West with her husband and had returned when he died. A popular and morally faultless lady who had taught many of the children and adults of the district, she had received a rating of "second," or "good," from previous supervisors. Parker rated her sixth, or "bad, very bad." His district committee, allegedly now completely under his sway, agreed to fire Mrs. Isbell summarily. Then the series of moves Parker had planned became clear. Miss Freeman of the Poplar Street School was to take Mrs. Isbell's place; the place of Miss Freeman was to be filled by Miss Kendrick of the Prince School, and into the now vacant position in the demonstration school was to go Parker's favorite from Quincy. An additional complication was Parker's admission that his Quincy teacher "could not compete with girls from the high and normal schools" in the standard teacher's examination, a problem he overcame by bullying the committee to waive the test.　　*146304*

The firing of Mrs. Isbell was too much for both the opponents of Parker and the residents of the Blossom Street district. They tried unsuccessfully to persuade the school committee to reinstate Mrs. Isbell. A number of "the most worthy citizens of West Boston protested, and a petition, signed by

Reverend C. A. Bartol, Alderman Slade, Thomas Gaffield [a retired merchant], F. T. Connell and others was sent to the School Board for a hearing." Under pressure from many people, the board had little choice, and as its hearing into the dismissal of Mrs. Isbell proceeded the full facts of the case emerged for the first time.

The hearing itself turned into a violent attack on Parker, led by Gaffield, and resulted in a thorough public condemnation of Parker. He had gone too far. Amid the bureaucratic uniformity of the Boston school system his individualistic style, his contempt for regulations and standard operating procedures, emerged in a harsh and glaring light. After the facts became public at the hearing, the school board had little choice, and only Brooks Adams supported Parker. The board officially reinstated Mrs. Isbell in her school; Parker had been beaten.

It is not surprising that Parker soon left Boston. Parker was a man who simply could not tolerate the climate of an urban school system, and the system really could not tolerate him. Parker had to be able to control and transform any organization of which he was a member. Talented, egotistic, and ambitious, he could not brook opposition, delay, or the frustrations of trying to reform urban schools. He was the sort of man who works well in a small town or city like Quincy or, even better, in a normal school, where his influence could extend to every member. Parker's experience in Boston revealed the incompatibility of charisma and bureaucracy; it showed up the utopianism of those who proclaimed that a single enlightened and magnetic man could transform a large urban school system; and it provided evidence that even Charles Francis Adams, Jr., the most realistic critic of the time, had not given urban schools an alternative to rigid and formalistic bureaucracy. Essentially it was on charismatic bureaucracy that the Boston reformers had placed their hopes: Able outsiders hired as supervisors were to break the grip of the masters and, by their personal influence, reform the temper of the schools. One reason the reformers failed was their reliance on this implausible scheme.

By the end of 1881 it was clear that the direction of events within the Boston school system was still changing in favor of the masters and their supporters. For one thing, prosperity had returned, and the need for economizing was no longer urgent. At the city Democratic convention in 1881, only the chairman's vote renominated Brooks Adams for the school board; with this evidence of dissatisfaction, he withdrew. The withdrawal of Adams and the election of Gaffield, the retired merchant who was Mrs. Isbell's knight, symbolized the shift of educational opinion, reflected, too, in the letters to newspapers calling for a return to the old system. Some of the letters came from Philbrick, who, sensing that the city was ripe for change, vitriolically denounced the school board members and called on the voters to turn them out of office *en masse*.

Although only four of its twelve recently elected members were new, the school board of 1882 gave indications from the beginning of the year that change was imminent. Predictably, in early February members of the school board offered two motions, one to return the principalship of the primary schools to the grammar school masters, and the other to subordinate the supervisors to the superintendent by making them assistant superintendents.

The supporters of the schoolmen were not slow to point out the significance of the vote at which the former recommendation, with only slight modification, was passed. One called it clear proof that John Dudley Philbrick had been right all the time. The editor of the *Journal of Education* termed the restoration a vindication of the "old regime" and proclaimed that the teachers of the city found it a "famous victory." Despite their weak, untenured position, the masters had shown their real strength; the struggle and their eventual victory demonstrated that the day had passed when a school committee could impose reform without the support of its teaching staff. Alienated by the reform movement, the masters, with the support of the *Journal of Education*, had effectively prevented the successful operation of the "new departure." An influential and cohesive unofficial group within the larger school system, the masters had proved that without their approval no school policy could succeed. The reformers, blind to the constraints that impede changes within complex organizations, had failed to realize the potency of the masters and had blithely proceeded to innovate with full confidence that, as the legal masters of the system, they could work changes at will. They learned otherwise, as has each succeeding generation of reformers ever since.

Although no substantive changes were introduced during the next year, 1883, restoration of harmony continued, and the good feelings proved not to be transient. Comments from even formerly hostile sources underlined the transformed atmosphere described by the board. Really, all that remained for the counterrevolution was to make the superintendent in law—according to the regulations, that is—the true head of the school system. When this happened at last in 1884, the Boston bureaucracy was truly complete. The centralization and addition of supervisory personnel effected by the 1876 reorganization had run counter to the principles underlying bureaucracies in some critical ways. They had left the definition of roles unclear and assigned the same administrative duties to different individuals. Instead of a smoothly efficient hierarchy, the changes had introduced confusion and controversy into the school system. Reformers, moreover, had violated bureaucratic canons by appointing laymen to high office instead of promoting them from the ranks. Now, at least, these problems had been solved. The supervisors had been given a definite place in the hierarchy; functions had been differentiated more clearly; control had been centralized more firmly; some Boston masters had even been elected supervisors. The anomalies that made bureaucracy only incipient in the plans of Henry Barnard or in towns like Quincy had been removed. In fact as well as on paper, the Boston school system had become a proper bureaucracy. Other American cities soon followed its example.

One consequence of bureaucratization, Amitai Etzioni has pointed out, is the separation of consumption, those who are served by an organization, from control, those who direct it. This distinction points up a significant aspect of the bureaucratization of American urban education: the altered relation of the school to the community. As the organization of urban education became more complex, schools were increasingly divorced from the communities they served, and laymen had progressively less power to influence school policy. In turn, schoolmen themselves gained augmented power to run the schools as they saw fit, with little or no reference to the actual requirements of the community. From one point of view, it certainly was desirable for career educators to acquire the autonomy necessary to free them from meddling and uninformed interference. But from another point of view, the ability to resist community opinion, revealed by the success of the Boston masters against the reformers, contributed to the sterility of urban education. Needing to communicate only with one another, with many legitimate concerns for their own status, power, and protection, schoolmen, whenever attacked, have been quick to withdraw into the protective shell of their massive school systems. Bureaucratization has lessened their sensitivity to their communities, to their students, and to the informed and constructive criticism that would make progress possible. The reaction of schoolmen to the voice of lay criticism became a defensive reflex as the traditions of resistance forming in the nineteenth century calcified into hardened and ingrained responses.

The conflicting needs for both autonomy and responsiveness in educational systems was one dilemma posed by the bureaucratization of education. Another was the problem of finding an alternative model of educational organization. For the most part, the alternatives that seemed alive in 1850 no longer appeared viable in 1875. During the later nineteenth century, perceptive critics were fully aware that public education required some form of rational organization. They clearly saw the tension between vitality and responsiveness, on the one hand, and the demands of a complex administrative task, on the other. Knowing that they could not dispense with formal structure, they still looked for alternatives to the rigidly hierarchical models that had emerged. But all proposed solutions were inadequate; no one had a viable alternative. The problem has not disappeared. Critics of the schools have continued to lament their rigid and formalistic features, their negative influence on the personality of teachers and students, their inability to accommodate highly individualistic styles of conduct. But an organizational alternative to overcome these deficiencies is still to be formulated; despite nearly a century of criticism, American education still lacks a real alternative model to hierarchical bureaucracy.

3

Twentieth-Century School Reform: Notes Toward a History*

The structure of American urban education has not changed since late in the nineteenth century; by 1880, the basic features of public education in most major cities were the same as they are today. The absence of those characteristics in some places did not reflect a different pattern of educational development; it represented, rather, a slower rate of urban growth. In time these places too acquired the distinctive marks of American urban education.

Continuities in Educational Structure

Beyond doubt, there have been educational developments and innovations of first-rate importance since the late nineteenth century. Consider, for instance, the kindergarten, the junior high school, industrial education, testing, the new math. Each has brought about change; but—and this is the

* Parts of this chapter, in a slightly different form, appeared in a review of Gross and Gross, eds., *Radical School Reform* (copyright 1970 Saturday Review, Inc.) and are reprinted here by permission of the *Saturday Review*.

important point—it is change *within* a given structure that itself has not altered. That is the basis on which we can claim continuity in American education over almost a century.

What were the features fixed so firmly by the late nineteenth century? Most succinctly, public education was universal, tax-supported, free, compulsory, bureaucratically arranged, class-biased, and racist. That those characteristics existed by 1880 should be evident from the preceding chapters. Their continuity is not hard to demonstrate.

By 1880 most people went to school for at least some period of time. The enormous expansion of high school enrollment in the early twentieth century did not represent a break with tradition but, rather, the continuation and acceleration of a trend that had been in motion since at least the middle of the nineteenth century. Continuous increase in the average school-leaving age has been a pronounced feature of educational history, and waves of attendance have swept upward through the common school, through the high school, and now, nearly, through the college.

Continuities in finance appear even more clearly than in attendance patterns. Despite well-documented inadequacies, property taxation remains the principal source of educational revenue, and gross inequalities continue to mark different regions and even neighboring communities. The federal funding provided by the Elementary and Secondary Education Act of 1965 in principle represents a significant departure in school finance, but the sums it has provided thus far are pitifully small compared to the total cost of education.

Similarly, education has remained free. In fact, like school attendance, the scope of free education has expanded. The significant debate has moved, over the course of a century, from the propriety of providing free common schools to free high schools and, now, to free higher education. It is carried on within the framework of the assumption that the public should provide and pay for a complete system of formal schooling. There is controversy about the limits of that system, but the assumption, injected with such force into public consciousness by mid-nineteenth-century schoolmen, remains unchallenged.

Nor has the compulsory nature of schooling changed. By the late nineteenth century the public in most places had accepted the concept of compulsion, although the enforcement of compulsory laws remained uncertain and inefficient. Compulsion had followed with inexorable logic from the expectations people had for their schools and from the relationship they perceived between schooling and public welfare, as I hope the earlier discussion has made clear. Its diffusion is evidence, once more, of the similarity of educational purpose and organization throughout the country. Compulsion has become woven into the structure of education and into the popular mind; it is no longer a radical solution to a problem but part of the conventional wisdom, as the following incident illustrates. Only a few years ago the Massachusetts legislature passed a comprehensive new school law and, in the process, repealed all the old laws. The day after passage, to the dismay of the legislature, it was discovered that compulsory education had been repealed unwittingly. Immediately, the governor drafted a bill; it passed the legislature at once and without demur.

As we have seen, the Boston school system had become a bureaucracy, in every sense of that term, by 1875. By that date, other school systems had become bureaucratic as well, and those that had not followed their example by early in the twentieth century. It is not necessary to point out the extent to which bureaucracy remains the organizational form of urban education today. What is of particular interest about the contemporary situation is that bureaucracy itself has become an objective of reform assault, as it has not been for some time. But contemporary attempts to reduce the bureaucratic element in urban education appear to be no more successful than earlier ones were, and the problems that frustrated and finally defeated the Boston School Committee and Francis Parker in the late 1870's seem as prominent today as then.

Formulation of the relationships between bureaucracy and class bias remains a major task of social historians and social theorists. My earlier discussion of incipient bureaucratic models and of the mediating function of organizations represents only a beginning. Nevertheless, although we lack an adequate statement of relationships, we can be quite sure that some connection did exist. We have seen that bureaucratic forms developed early in the history of public schooling; we have observed as well that class bias was reflected in the educational aims of the same period. Bureaucracy was the form of organization best suited to the realization of those aims, and it is in this fact that the relationship between class and bureaucracy lies. Sociological and administrative theory generally assumes a functional—and, implicitly, inevitable—relationship between urban industrial society and bureaucratic organization. Given the complexity of society, it is believed, business cannot be arranged otherwise. However, it is not impossible to imagine different arrangements for social institutions, such as schools, as contemporary exponents of decentralization are proving. In fact, bureaucracy is inevitable only if social complexity is approached with certain particular values and priorities. If order, efficiency, and uniformity are preferred to responsiveness, variety, and flexibility, then, indeed, bureaucracy is inevitable.

But order, efficiency, and uniformity, values that have permeated public education since the nineteenth century, have strong class overtones. That has been shown in a variety of ways in the preceding chapters. Perhaps the strongest impulse behind the founding of public educational systems was what today we would call the urge for law and order, or the attempt to socialize the urban poor to behavior that will decrease crime, diminish expenditures on public welfare, promote safety on the streets, and contribute to industrial productivity. Early school promoters convinced their constituencies that public education would accomplish those ends, and their imminent attainment has been confidently predicted ever since. Despite overwhelming disconfirming evidence, faith in the power—the essentially conservative power—of schooling has persisted, and this is one of the great puzzles in the history of American thought.

One reason relates to the problem of finding nonsocialist approaches to social reform. An official ideology that emphasizes the importance of free enterprise and shuns state intervention has limited alternatives with which to approach major social problems, such as poverty. Massive income redistribution or broad-scale intervention in the economy generally has not been acceptable. Education, on the other hand, has appeared to be an immediate and effective solution to social problems. There is a surface logic, which remains immensely appealing: Equipping children with appropriate skills and attitudes can cause the problems of unemployment and poverty to disappear. The illnesses of society become diagnosed as simply a lack of education, and the prescription for reform becomes more education. The prescription, for one thing, unleashes a flurry of seemingly purposeful activity and, for another, requires no tampering with basic social structural or economic characteristics, only with the attitudes of poor people, and that has caused hardly a quiver. The problem (and the determination with which people have refused to admit it is powerful testimony to the usefulness of the idea) is that this approach to social reform simply has not worked. In fact, insofar as it has been a smoke screen, obscuring the nature of social problems, educational reform has hindered broader social reform.

The other reason that the power of schooling has remained an article of faith rests on the class bias inherent in the actual structure and functioning of school systems. Educational rhetoric to the contrary notwithstanding, it is the children of the well-to-do, not the children of the poor, who have benefited most from public education. That is especially true of the higher levels of schooling, one important function of which has been to secure differential advantage to the children of the affluent. Throughout the history of education there have been essentially two levels of schooling: one virtually universal, and the other attended by a minority of the eligible children. There is, as I said earlier, little evidence to point out where that minority came from, but what there is indicates that it was largely the children of the affluent. When the common school had become universal, for instance, the children who attended high school represented the more prosperous sections of the community. Today, when high school is virtually universal, the same is true of the students at public universities.

This means that the continuous extension of educational facilities has been, and continues to be, primarily in the interests of the affluent in a very direct and immediate sense. That extension first of all spreads to the community as a whole the financial burden of providing a minority, and a select minority, of the children with an economic advantage over the rest. At the same time, it operates as a continuous social sorting device enabling well-to-do children to retain or improve their advantage while doing very little for the rest. The notion that schooling secures differential advantages to the poor covers this situation very nicely.

Public education represents a social sorting device stacked even more heavily against blacks than against the poor. Racism remains as integral and functional to public education as ever. An attitude that describes one group of people as essentially different from, and inferior to, the dominant group is racist. From this perspective, as I have argued earlier, racism underlay the origins of public education; for the poor, especially the Irish Catholic poor, appeared to school promoters in exactly those terms. The racism implicit in the origins of public education became functional as an excuse for educational failure. Newly created systems of public education failed to meet the ends for which they had been established, and some explanation became necessary. The same problem faced the managers of newly created reform schools, prisons, and mental hospitals. In each case, including that of public education, they created a defense in terms of the inferiority of their inmates. That inferiority, it was argued, was hereditary; thus, given the inferior stock with which they had to contend, what could one expect?

Thought about education, crime, mental illness, and delinquency has oscillated between stresses on environment and on heredity. Both have had racist implications, the latter more blatantly. Generally speaking, environmentalism has been optimistic and hence characteristic of movements of reform. Thus it dominated reform thought in the 1840's and surfaced again at the end of the century and in the early 1960's. In each case, the reappearance of an emphasis on heredity has accompanied the frustration of reformist expectations and the waning of reformist zeal. That happend in the 1860's and again in the early twentieth century; it happened again in 1969, when Arthur R. Jensen, a leading educational psychologist, published an influential article ascribing lower native intelligence to blacks than to whites. The article followed and built upon the vaguely pessimistic conclusions of the Coleman report on *Equality of Educational Opportunity* that the quality of schooling does not matter and of the Commission on Civil Rights on *Racial Isolation in the Public Schools* that compensatory education has failed. Jensen's thesis has been eagerly seized upon by a variety of strange bedfellows, from Southern white supremacists to big-city school people anxious to excuse their own ineptitude.

The racism sometimes inherent in the environmentalist position (where environment is defined as the *family* context) is more subtle, and for that reason often more insidious. Its genteel wrapping covers its animus; the general tone is pity for the deprived slum child, who lacks opportunities to learn manners and morals, to see cows and trees, to learn long words and respect for education. The bias in this attitude is apparent on a moment's reflection, as the following example should make clear: It is considered an instance of cultural deprivation if a slum child cannot identify a cow but not if a suburban child is unable to identify a cockroach. This attitude strenuously avoids condemning the child and places the blame on his background. It views the job of the school as massively compensatory. In one form or another, the argument has been put forward since the nineteenth century. Its sponsors consistently have failed to see that it is condescending and patronizing, or offensive, to the poor themselves. Two ways in which it is particularly insidious should be observed; first of all, it teaches the child to regard his parents and his home with an emotion ranging between pity and contempt. Second, it removes responsibility for educational failure from the teacher and school fully as much as the hereditary position. Translated into practical terms, the environmental position also permits the school to excuse itself, or to lessen its effort, in view of the homes from which the students come. Given all those obstacles of environment, the well-meaning liberal teacher might well ask, what can I be expected to do?

Today, obviously, the notion of cultural deprivation expresses the environmentalist point of view. Although its proponents sometimes assume that their concept is novel, in fact it stretches back well into the nineteenth century. The image of the poor in educational thought has shifted from the depraved to the deprived during the last century; the basis of the argument has moved from moralism to social psychology. But the direction, the animus, and—need it be stressed—the racism remain.

Urban public school systems present a curious amalgam of inherent structural and ideological defects; it is no wonder that they have failed. They have not reformed society; they have not won the allegiance of the poor and the black; they have not bound Americans to each other in affection and respect. They have been erected first and foremost upon a soft, evasive intellectual base; they have depended on a continued reluctance to compare their actual and official functions or their stated and operative purposes. They have developed organizational structures that moved them ever farther away from interaction with the communities they served, and, finally, they have even refused to accept responsibility for educating anybody successfully in anything. Once granted a captive audience, they have had little need to succeed; it has been easier to develop a battery of excuses that place the blame for educational failure outside the school and on the home.

This situation immediately raises another historical problem: Why have reform movements failed to change these characteristics of urban education? In particular, what of progressive education? The answer to that question is implicit in what I have written already. It is sad but true that an understanding of earlier reform efforts and their failures permits us to make general predictions about others. Of the reform thrust known as progressivism in the late nineteenth and early twentieth centuries I have said little, quite deliberately. My contention is that the shape of public education in American cities had been fixed before progressivism began. Progressivism failed to alter that shape. It failed partly because it suffered from the weaknesses of earlier reform movements. It failed as well because it did not even try. For the most part, progressivism represented a conservative movement that accepted the structure of American education as it was and tried to work changes within that framework.

Progressivism and Education

The term "progressive education" immediately conjures up a host of images: John Dewey, the child-centered school, the project method, Auntie Mame. But to accept those images uncritically would be a drastic oversimplification. Progressive is an umbrella label, and not a very satisfactory one at that, for a wide variety of activities directed toward changing American political and institutional behavior between, roughly, 1890 and World War I. The relations between reform efforts in education and in other places are intimate, complex, and hardly disentangled yet by historians. In education alone, progressivism refers to activities on a variety of planes; sometimes they overlapped, sometimes they remained quite separate. But any comprehensive analysis of progressivism must include them all. Most succinctly, they are (1) the attempt to alter the political control of education, (2) the reformulation of educational thought, (3) the introduction of educational innovations, (4) the promotion of pedagogical change, and (5) the injection of scientific management into administrative practice.

At this juncture, discussion of these activities and their interrelationships must be more or less speculative. Historians have done astoundingly little research on any of them, with the possible exception of educational thought, and even there they have largely confined themselves to leading theorists and neglected the attitudes of teachers, administrators, and various public groups. They have neglected, even more, the working out of reform efforts on the local level. Consequently, we have almost no case studies that trace attitudes and developments in particular communities and try to find out exactly what sorts of change happened in schools. Some, although woefully little, work on these topics has begun in the last few years, and the first results are just appearing. Thus, it is peculiarly difficult to write meaningfully about educational reform in the progressive period. What follows, therefore, is a series of hunches about how the history of that period will look when the evidence is in.

At one level, progressivism meant municipal reform; that was the case for both city politics and education. Throughout the country, coalitions of urban reformers tried to replace the bosses who governed American cities, to reform the legal structure of city government, and to increase the efficiency of municipal services. Their campaigns combined moral indignation at corruption with a protest at the high cost of graft and inefficiency, and in city after city they exposed major scandals. Education formed part of the municipal system that needed cleaning up. School systems provided patronage in the form of jobs, contracts, and supplies, and city political machines had not been backward about exploiting their potential. As part of their effort to improve municipal government, reformers sought to change the nature and source of educational control. For the most part, they proposed the centralization of power in a small school board with members elected at large. That would replace the large boards with members elected from wards, and it was ward politics that was particularly associated with political machines. A small central board representing the entire city, reformers felt, would be more independent of political influences. It would be the job of the new board to introduce the regulations and procedures that would replace nepotism and graft with equity, efficiency, and good business practices.

Two features of this reform are especially relevant to the analysis of progressivism in education. First, it reflected very little concern for children. Political and economic considerations dominated the movement; educational ones remained quite marginal. Second, it represented a class effort. The small amount of historical work that has been done on the composition of reform groups finds them largely controlled by old-stock first citizens, quite often professionals. Municipal reform represented as much a thrust for power by this group as it did a moral crusade for good government. Bossism, ward politics, and immigrants were linked together in public attitudes. Consequently, an anti-immigrant and anti-working-class attitude underlay much of municipal reform. It would be instructive to analyze overlapping membership in municipal-reform and immigrant-restriction associations; I suspect it would be substantial.

Educational reform reflected these biases. The men and women concerned with altering the control of education had no higher opinion of poor city families than did their predecessors a half-century before. They shared the anti-immigrant sentiments and the racism of their class. Insofar as their reform efforts had an educational purpose, that goal again reflected one of the larger aims of municipal reform: the attempt to find new modes of social control appropriate to a dynamic and fluid urban environment. Their aim remained similar to that of earlier reformers: inculcating the poor with acceptable social attitudes. This has had important implications. It has meant that the government of school systems has continued to rest on a disdain for a large portion of students and their families. This has only widened the gulf between working-class communities and schools that mid-century reformers had helped to create. Schools remained distant and alien institutions to the poor, the bureaucratic detachment of the staff reinforced by the bias of those in political control of the system.

It is the tradition of distance and disdain that has led to the confrontation between black communities and school systems in recent times. The hostile reaction of school boards like Boston's in the 1960's to the problem of *de facto* segregation, for instance, revealed how the long-standing insensitivity of a school system to its poorer clientele had hardened into a pattern of interacting with community groups. Incident after incident suggested that the school board simply did not care to try to understand the aspirations of some black people; it appeared, very simply, that the wishes of black people did not matter much. That open confrontation has now broken out in some areas should surprise no one. It is the legacy of school government cut off from and insensitive to the community it serves.

The relationship between municipal reform and the formulation of educational theory remains to be explored. As it is usually understood, progressive educational thought appears to be radically different in tone and intention from the movement for political control. Professor Lawrence Cremin, in *Transformation of the School*, has provided a sympathetic and incisive intellectual history of progressive thought that reinforces its traditional image. The difficulty with Cremin's version is its inability to relate theory to action, to connect politics with educational reform. For Cremin portrays educational theory as broadly humane and democratic—even, at times, libertarian. It lacks, in his account, the impulse to social control and social order apparent in progressive political activity. According to Cremin, educational progressivism was a branch of political progressivism, and he views the latter as moved by the same generous impulses as the educational theory he describes. The problem lies in his version of political progressivism, which historians are steadily replacing with one similar to the interpretation sketched above. Either educational theory and political reform developed along different lines, or the interpretation of that theory must undergo a revision comparable to the interpretation of other aspects of reform.

As we have come to view it, progressive educational thought stressed the incorporation of the experience of the child into the development of the curriculum, the softening of pedagogy, the breaking down of barriers between subjects, and the active participation of the learner. At its best, as in Dewey's formulation, educational theory combined a focus on the child and his world with a driving social-reformist commitment that, in the tradition of American educational thought, saw education as the key to social uplift.

The child-centered and the social reformist are two of the important strands in progressive educational thought. A third is the scientific. At times the three strands coexisted, as in the writings of Dewey; at other times strains between priorities drove them apart. The scientific assumed an independent existence most notably. Educational psychology, in particular, lost the broad social and philosophic concerns apparent in the writings of early theorists, especially Dewey, and narrowed its focus, concentrating on testing and the measurement of individual differences. The IQ test and the abuses of measurement remain heirs to the progressive tradition in education and, indeed, in American thought, fully as much as the contemporary movement for free schools. Progressive reformers of all varieties attempted to utilize the methods and findings of science in the promotion of their goals.

Dewey, it is true, resisted the increasing divorce of science and philosophy in educational theory as well as the other sectarian excesses of progressive educators. Nonetheless, there is a darker side to the social thought of even the best progressives, notably Dewey and Jane Addams, and it is that aspect of their writing that is congruent with the impulses at work in municipal reform. The point is complex, and it has just begun to be developed by historians, particularly Clarence Karier and Paul Violas. Briefly, the emphasis on community in Jane Addams and the definitions of democracy and experience in Dewey provide particularly subtle and sophisticated instances of the widespread attempt in their time to foster modes of social control appropriate to a complex urban environment. Most starkly, both Addams and Dewey in the last analysis stressed the subservience of individual will and aspiration to those of the group. Dewey's educational ideal, it has been pointed out often enough, did not leave the child unregulated and alone; it retained a strong guiding role for the teacher. That role became largely the creation of an environment, a carefully planned group context that would provide children with a sequence of experiences, which, despite their apparent spontaneity, were in fact meticulously elicited. Those experiences would lead the children to develop habitual ways of responding, to internalize the norms of democratic living. The key to democracy for Dewey was in action; democracy was not a static form but a mode of living, a way of behaving in which each person continually referred his actions and his desires to the well-being of the group. Education, by implication, served to instill conformist behavior, a set of inner controls that would make external social controls unnecessary. This for Jane Addams was the function of community. Both she and Dewey were acutely conscious of the decline of traditional social controls in urban and industrial settings; both saw a need to accommodate industrial workers to their work. They emphasized the importance of teaching assembly-line workers the importance of their task and its place in the larger processes of production. This was, as it is usually presented, an effort to relieve the tedium and mental drudgery of manual work. But its larger social function, the result if it worked, would be to socialize workers to contentment and to increase their identification with their industry.

Despite their subtle coercive implications, Dewey's educational proposals represented a vast improvement over most contemporary practice. Unfortunately, he did little to implement their adoption other than to establish a model school. In fact, his writings generally fail to deal with the relationship between the structure of school systems and the content of education. He did not ask, that is, whether it was possible to effect a reform of pedagogy within the bureaucratic structure of urban schools. That question was left largely unexplored by progressive theorists, which is one of the central weaknesses of their writings. For, if radical structural alteration must precede significant pedagogical change, then the first efforts of school reformers must be directed toward breaking down the bureaucratic form of schooling and changing the nature of its political control. That this is the case certainly forms part of the argument of educational radicals today, a point to which I shall return. Whether or not the point is valid, it is one with which serious educational theory must grapple, as the progressives did not.

It should be clear that to study the writing of leading educational theorists is not to learn what goes on in school. This has probably always been the case, and the progressive period is no exception. Did pedagogy change during the progressive period? If it did, did the impulse come from progressive theory or some other source? Historians, as I have pointed out, cannot answer these questions. They know that certain things happened—the introduction of industrial education, the kindergarten, and guidance; the development of ability grouping; the creation of "social studies"; the use in some places of movable furniture and the project method. But our knowledge, even about these tangible innovations, is vague. In how many places, for instance, was the project method used? What sorts of schools introduced guidance counselors first?

Even if we grant that a number of innovations entered schoolrooms and school systems, we still must ask about more fundamental issues. Had the attitudes of teachers altered? Was school in general a friendlier, happier place? Had there been an improvement in the relationship between the school and its community? I suspect the answers to these questions, when we learn them, will be negative. In fact, the significance of the changes that did occur is that they represent an outgrowth of long-standing concerns and well-established patterns, not new departures, and not the influence of progressive educational theory.

Consider, for instance, the introduction of industrial education. Relating the school to industrial employment had been a concern of many people, including employers' groups, for a long time. The argument that schooling was insuffici-

ently practical and that it paid too much attention to the head
and too little to the hand was not especially theoretical. For a
long time, though, advocates of directly vocational training
made little headway, and it was only toward the end of the
nineteenth century that they scored significant gains. The
timing of their success is suggestive; it coincides with both
heavy immigration and the increase in high school enrollment. It is possible to suppose that industrial education appeared to be a handy solution to the problem of catering to
large numbers of less able or less academic students. It was
also a solution fit for poor children; it would permit them to
attend secondary school without imbibing aspirations beyond
their class. It would continue to instill in them the attitudes
and skills appropriate to manual working-class status. Regardless of the rhetoric of its sponsors, industrial education has
proved to be an ingenious way of providing universal secondary schooling without disturbing the shape of the social
structure and without permitting excessive amounts of social
mobility.

A similar hypothesis accounts for the origin and spread of
the kindergarten. Early childhood education has a long history,
dating from the infant school movement in late-eighteenth-
century England. At that time philanthropists, concerned with
the problem of juvenile crime, urged the establishment of
schools for very young children, aged two or three. The purpose of such institutions was to counteract the unfavorable
moral environment of the home, which, it was argued, led to
delinquent and later criminal behavior. Although the infant
school movement failed to spread widely in America, its emphasis on early childhood education became a permanent feature of educational thought. Later schoolmen, including those
of the mid-nineteenth century, developed that emphasis. They,
too, stressed the importance of counteracting the unfavorable
influence of the home and argued that the primary purpose
of early education was the formation of attitudes rather than

the development of skills. It was this emphasis on the relationship of early childhood education to social order that fed the kindergarten movement, in the same way, quite obviously, that widespread concern with crime and welfare expenses have given impetus to movements for preschool education today.

Industrial education and the kindergarten represent outgrowths of the traditional conservative impulse at the basis of educational change. Other innovations, while reflecting that impulse as well, represent extensions of bureaucratic structure. These are ability grouping, the junior high school, and guidance. Each represented the introduction of one more specialized component into an increasingly subdivided, hierarchical form of organization. Each represented an extension of the already existing pattern of bureaucratic development, not a change of direction.

Guidance and ability grouping are also of interest because they too have functioned, despite their stated purposes, as social sorting devices. They have legitimized a way of channeling working-class children into working-class jobs; they have utilized the mantle of science to disguise the fact that schools reinforce existing patterns of social structure. Here the interrelationship between bureaucratic structure and class bias becomes especially clear. Bureaucracy provides a segmented educational structure that legitimizes and perpetuates the separation of children along class lines and ensures easier access to higher-status jobs for children of the affluent.

This is my hypothesis. The evidence to support it fully has not yet been compiled, but it is not inconsistent with the facts as they are known. It is a hypothesis about the function of educational innovations as distinct from their explicit purposes. It holds, in fact, that there is often a discrepancy between the two. As it relates to progressivism in education, the hypothesis maintains that most progressive innovations, so-called, operated as social sorting mechanisms supportive of existing social patterns and social inequalities. Despite the rhetoric of their sponsors, progressive innovations inhibited rather than fostered social change and social reform. Like the educational reform movement of the mid-nineteenth century, progressivism was profoundly conservative, for it sprang from a search for social order.

The attitudes of the men who directed educational change, city superintendents and professors of education, underlines the essentially conservative nature of progressivism. Once again, it is important to recall that historians have been remarkably slow about systematically studying the social attitudes of school administrators, but the little we do know suggests that they were strongly committed to bureaucratic forms and frequently racist in outlook. Certainly, the lessons that school administrators learned from the most eminent professors of education had conservative biases, as a study of the work of David Snedden, the virtual founder of educational sociology, or of Elwood Cubberly, a profoundly influential teacher of administration, reveals. Cubberly taught and wrote on the subject of administration and on educational history as well; his influence spread not only through those endeavors but also through the surveys of city school systems that he conducted. David Tyack has made it quite clear that Cubberly believed in the inferiority of new immigrant groups. Although Cubberly criticized school practice, his proposals for reform did not call as much for a change of structure or direction as for a more streamlined bureaucracy. What he proposed for the improvement of urban school systems was greater centralization, more professional control, and increased efficiency in operation.

An emphasis on efficiency permeated educational writing, and, indeed, reform writing in other fields as well, with monotonous regularity. Efficiency, as in the case examined earlier, continued to imply the application of scientific methods to simultaneously improve quality and lower costs. Raymond

Callahan has argued that the emphasis on efficiency, particularly scientific management, represented an almost conspiratorial attempt to foist business values on the school. That is stretching the point. It would be more accurate to say that the conduct of both social, including educational, reform and of business shared values that were prominent in American society, and that the men who ran schools differed little in their attitudes and outlook from the men who ran businesses. Whether an innovation appears to be progressive or regressive depends on the perspective of the observer. Thus, Lawrence Cremin considers the innovations in the schools of Gary, Indiana, to be the quintessence of progressivism, because they represented a wholehearted attempt to improve the practice of education within a city school system. Raymond Callahan, on the other hand, regards the Gary system as proof of the misapplication of scientific management in education because it represented an attempt to cut costs. Both historians are right, in a sense. Gary provides an excellent illustration of the dominant impulse of the period: the effort to obtain improvement and economy through the use of science.

If Robert and Helen Lynd were right and Middletown did represent a typical American city, then its educational history supports the arguments that I have advanced in this section. There, in the 1920's, the Lynds found an educational system virtually untouched by the theory and ferment of the preceding three decades. The school day in 1925 was rigid, dull, and routine, much as it must have been in 1890. In the intervening years the major changes had been the introduction of vocational courses, a heightened emphasis on the teaching of patriotism and civics, a blossoming of extracurricular activities, and the addition of more administrative personnel in the elaboration of the educational hierarchy. The school, however, remained, "like the factory," a "thoroughly regimented world." It was, in fact, in the 1930's, during the Depression, that the system changed most. The result of that change, to use Tyack's phrase, was a streamlined bureaucracy. The introduction of testing and guidance, the refinement of differences between schools, and of the professional self-consciousness of school people, the introduction of a research department, an assertion of the importance of individual differences, new curricula, an efficiency movement—these were some of the major changes. At the same time the expectations of the community remained the same, heightened, in fact, by the dislocations of the Depression. The schools were to continue to serve as a source of social order, stability, and the inculcation of patriotism. In short, Middletown's schools remained the same conservative, stabilizing institutions they had always been, now refurbished in modern form.

Progressive reforms touched Middletown late, and they touched it superficially. This was the usual course of events. Partly, the force of tradition, the resistance of educators to change, and the conservative expectations of communities all combined to frustrate educational reform. But that is not the entire story, as I hope this section has made clear. Progressive reform, even at its most articulate, did not challenge social or institutional structure. At its most typical it sought reforms profoundly congruent with the conservative commercial ethos at the heart of American life. Progressivism did not fail to work a fundamental transformation in American schools; it did not even try.

The Present Moment in Educational Reform

What of the current movement for educational reform? In what ways does it resemble those of the past? Is there any reason to believe that its results will be more fundamental? The parallels between the present and the past are implicit in what I have written so far. We are today experiencing the third major movement for urban educational reform in American history. Like those of the mid-nineteenth century and the progressive period, it is a part of a larger movement to improve the quality of urban life. But I use the present tense with some trepidation. For, as I write this, late in 1970, I think the drive and dynamism have gone. The indicator, as I pointed out earlier, was the re-emergence of emphasis on the role of heredity in educational achievement. Twice before, this kind of event signaled the waning of reformist energy; perhaps it has done so once again.

The current movement began partly with the traditional conservative concern about crime and social disorder on city streets; it intertwined with the thrust for civil rights, and the combination gave it, initially, enormous power. At the start, integration provided a great moral issue that united blacks, whites, liberals, radicals, and even many conservatives. That was early in the 1960's, and it seems now long ago, an arcadian era of wonderful simplicity. Two clear-cut goals emerged for education: improving urban schools, and ending *de facto* segregation. At the time they seemed to be possible, difficult but attainable. Compensatory education and integration provided the means with which reform began; it was a moment of great optimism. Since that time the tensions inherent in the movement have erupted. The strains and contradictions between integration and compensatory education, between integration and decentralization, and between radical pedagogical reform and community participation—these, to name but three, have driven wedges into the movement, fragmenting it into antagonistic pieces.

The parallels between the four models presented earlier and contemporary proposals for reform are striking. The least explicit is paternalistic voluntarism, but it is nonetheless present, underlying the idea that school boards should be formed of a small body of first citizens appointed by the mayor. The proposal rests, first, on the naive assumption, characteristic also of paternalistic voluntarists, that education can somehow be divorced from politics. It rests, too, on the familiar and elitist premise that there resides within the community a body of disinterested and wise citizens, devoid of political or personal motives, uniquely capable of identifying and implementing the public interest in education.

Corporate voluntarism has become a widely discussed alternative during the last few years. Its contemporary sponsors, such as Christopher Jencks, propose the replacement of the public monopoly of schooling with competing private groups operating their own institutions. The voucher system represents a popular version of this idea; its sponsors want to replace the direct funding of public schools with educational vouchers, financed, as now, by taxation, but cashable by parents or students at any school. Their model is classic liberal economics; the argument is that free competition among schools will foster quality education and that the fight for funds will produce both a variety of school types and a continuing effort to offer an education that is attractive to its customers. The contemporary proponents of corporate voluntarism argue that their proposals would put flexibility, variety, and a stimulus to improvement back into the conduct of education.

As in the mid-nineteenth century, democratic localism today is the most disputed alternative. Its advocates—for instance, in Ocean Hill–Brownsville—are the champions of community control; they propose the radical decentralization of city school systems into small districts governed by local community organizations. Their values are not dissimilar to those of Orestes Brownson; like him, they stress the virtues of a close relationship between school and community, the drawbacks of bureaucracy, and the relation of community control to democratic theory. They, too, distrust professionals. They seek a redistribution of power from the interests represented by central city governments to the poor and, in the case of ghetto people, to the black community itself. The search for black control of black institutions, especially schools, underlies much of the drive for community control. In this, too, there is a parallel between the present situation and the effort of the Irish Catholics in New York City to decentralize that city's system in the 1840's in order to gain control of the funds and institutions that provided schooling for their children.

Incipient bureaucracy likewise has its contemporary echoes. It might be more accurate, today, to speak of incipient technocracy. This variety of educational reform seeks to make changes within the existing educational system; it proposes sophisticated technological innovations to improve the content and procedures of schooling. Its most visible symbol is computer-assisted instruction. It is a point of view that does not feel uneasy about size; in fact, its proponents often advocate the creation of large educational parks that can economically incorporate the most advanced features of educational technology. Like the incipient bureaucrats of the last century, the technocrats stress the efficiency of their proposals and the increase in educational cost-benefit ratios that they will achieve. They likewise emphasize the importance of professionalism and the creation of new specialist roles within school systems. This approach to reform receives powerful support from two sources. One is from integrationists, who argue that only large educational parks drawing from a wide residential area can overcome the problem of *de facto* segregation based on housing. The other is professors of education; many support this approach, which assigns increased status and importance to their work and provides a justification for increased research funds.

With the exception of the technocrats, the proposals for reform that I have outlined stress structural changes, particularly the need to alter the political basis of educational control. In this there is an apparent similarity between the strivings of contemporary reformers and those of the progressive period. However, the direction of the movement is different today. The progressives, as we have seen, tried to centralize education; the main thrust of contemporary radical reform is toward decentralization. Two assumptions of the present movement deserve special attention. The first is that political change must precede educational change—that it is necessary to alter the political control of the school system before anything meaningful can change within the classroom. Second is the expectation that political change, meaning here the introduction of community control, will foster pedagogical reform; that it will mean children will receive a better education.

It is important to emphasize these assumptions because they, in turn, highlight the extent to which the movement for community control rests on particular value premises. It rests partly on the value that some black people attach to control of the education their children receive. Education controlled by whites, or reflecting white attitudes, they argue, by virtue of that fact cannot be adequate for black children. The other value position is the inherent worth that community control finds in close, almost symbiotic relations between institutions and the communities they serve. Community control, as much as earlier forms of educational organization, is a crystallization of certain values and priorities. Technocracy, for instance, gives priority to efficiency in terms of time and money, the attainment of intellectual skills, and professionalism. At one level, therefore, the differences between reform proposals are irreconcilable.

That is an important point, which contemporary debate obscures. Only some of the points at issue are open to discussion. Reformers, from one perspective, waste time talking to each other; they should put their proposals before the public, which eventually will have to choose between competing organizational forms and the values that they enshrine. Polemics, however, have only limited use; it would be more productive for proponents of differing viewpoints to identify the aspects of each other's positions that can in fact be challenged and discussed. The technocrats, for example, might ask the democrats to provide evidence that a change in the source of educational control will improve the content of schooling. The latter, in turn, might ask their antagonists to demonstrate the value of professionalism in education by, say, showing how graduate instruction in school administration improves the quality of education. Is there a relationship between the amount of graduate instruction given a school principal and the level at which the students in his school read and write?

One of the problems of contemporary reform is that people talk past each other, or else only to those already converted. The amount of good dialogue remains small. A second problem is the failure of the political and educational left honestly and hard-headedly to confront the value conflicts inherent within their own position. The left has become, in fact, tragically polarized, as the New York teachers' strike of 1968 demonstrated. The result has been dogmatic refusal to admit the ambiguities and contradictions within each position. One must, for instance, be either for or against community control. To be against, or to qualify one's comments, has come to be racist, an epithet that is clearly absurd if applied to men of unquestionably humane and democratic convictions, like Michael Harrington, who spoke on the side of the teachers.

It is not my intention to recount the events of the New York teachers strike or to try to untangle the web of charges and countercharges made by each side. There is ample documentation elsewhere, enough for readers to draw their own conclusions; I refer anyone interested, for a start, to Marilyn Gittell and Maurice Berube, *Confrontation at Ocean Hill–Brownsville*. I bring up the strike primarily to illustrate the dilemmas posed by community control, which supporters must confront but which, as I have said, are more obscured than dissected at present.

First of all, there is the problem of the teacher as a professional. In the early 1960's teacher unionism was a favorite cause with angry young graduate students in education and other educational radicals. These are the very people who today are among its strongest critics. But the arguments advanced in the early 1960's retain their validity. Teaching in America has always been poorly paid and poorly regarded. It is only recently that teachers have gained some measure of employment security and freedom from harassment and dismissal at the whim of school boards. Dreadful working conditions combined with the lack of autonomy, status, and adequate pay have sent people away from teaching in droves; it is a commonplace to observe that the brightest university graduates have not often entered the schools. Teacher unionism has been a response, and a very constructive one, to that problem.

Autonomy has been central to the problem. Even people who have been willing to accept a poor salary and who can remain indifferent to status have been repelled by the lack of autonomy, the rigid and petty authoritarian ethos of the schools. Bright, creative, and well-educated people want to function as professionals, to make the decisions about how they will do their job. Education has not suffered from any freedom granted teachers to run schools as they see fit; it has suffered from the suffocating atmosphere in which teachers have had to work. The popular attitude, and even that of reformers, equates the aims of administrators with those of teachers; it blames teachers for bureaucracy. The important point is that a distinction must be made; teachers do not run the schools. They are, as they will often tell you, harassed by the administration, which, if they are any good, continually gets in their way.

We have never had the situation in schools that we have in universities, where the faculty makes the educational decisions. Any attempted interference by governing boards with curriculum or pedagogy is greeted by academics, and justifiably, with appeals to academic freedom. In light of this, it is ironical, to say the least, that academics should support community control, at least as it has been advocated in Ocean

Hill–Brownsville, quite so uncritically. For, according to its by-laws, the governing board there retained to itself absolute power over all activities within the schools. What kind of educational change can be accomplished by exchanging one arbitrary educational authority for another?

It is ironical, too, that the teachers have opposed community control so uncreatively. They have sought not their freedom but their shelter in the protection of the bureaucracy. This, of course, reinforces the radical stereotype of the teacher as a rule-following servant of authority. On the radicals' side, too, is the unquestioned fact that many teachers are hostile to children, racist, or incompetent. Such teachers should be fired; they deserve no protection and no place in schools. Their protection by their colleagues and by the bureaucracy constitutes an enormous indictment of both.

It would be in the interests of both teachers and communities to develop a modified concept of decentralization and community school control. That concept would call for radically decentralized schools, each run by a coalition of teachers, parents, and students, much as the most progressive reformers are proposing for the restructuring of universities. Sensible divisions of authority, leaving to the teachers wide areas in which to exercise professional judgment, could be found. This sort of arrangement would offer the teachers the freedom to become professionals, which they now lack; it might also help to attract some independent-minded persons into teaching. It would offer communities decentralized schools and a meaningful role in their conduct. Students would gain the place in educational decision-making that they deserve, and the bureaucracy could be made obsolete. There would still be an important function for a teachers' union and equally, I think, for a union of students, who need to have their rights protected as well.

This is a straightforward way out of one of the conflicts that has troubled the decentralization movement (although I do not expect it would be easy to persuade the teachers' union to accept it). The other conflict appears to me less easy to resolve: the problem of integration. Community control and integration are incompatible, and for anyone who wants both that is a very hard fact to admit. Decentralized community schools must of necessity be small and local. In cities, that means that they must be within the ghettos; segregated residential patterns make it impossible for it to be otherwise. Nevertheless, integration is not impossible, as a number of people have argued; metropolitan cooperation in the creation of large educational parks could bring it about. Educational parks, however, would have to be large and formal, tightly administered, and distant from the communities they serve. At their best, they would be highly centralized, superlatively efficient, technologically advanced bureaucracies. They would decrease the possibilities of flexibility, variety, and community involvement. At their worst, they would be dreadful prisons, large repressive institutions with all the faults of contemporary urban schools magnified.

The Coleman report complicates the situation. It points, first, to the enormous disparity between white and black educational achievement. The median arithmetic score for black children graduating grade twelve is sixth grade. Reading is somewhat, but not much, better. Black and white children begin school not too far apart in test scores, but over time black scores fall and the differential increases. Part, and a very large part, of that cripplingly low educational achievement can be improved by integration; children segregated by social class or by race do much worse than those in integrated settings. Despite the weaknesses of the Coleman report, one finding appears undeniable: We could increase the educational achievement of black children substantially by sending them to schools in which a majority of the children are white. The same thing— and this is important, for it has the same implications for community control—is true of poor or lower-class children, despite their color. If they are sent to schools with a majority of middle-class students, their performance will improve. Moreover, it is not only academic achievement that will improve. The Coleman data show a substantial improvement in racial attitudes among students in integrated schools. White children who go to school with black children are more accepting, less racist, than those of comparable intelligence and status who attend all-white schools. Integration appears, then, to be a way to attack racist attitudes.

It is difficult, if not impossible, to conceive of a way of arranging schooling that permits integration, small size, and deep community involvement. That is the dilemma. Even if the goal of integration is abandoned—as it seems increasingly to be, with the sanction of both blacks and whites, though of course for different reasons—even in that case the problem of educational achievement remains. Reading and mathematics are skills that black children must learn as well as white and that in fact they do not now learn, for reasons that lie more within the school setting, it would appear, than within their homes. For, it seems to me, the Coleman data also suggest that the retarding influence of "impoverished" homes has been grossly overrated. Put in an integrated school context—that is, one more conducive to learning—black children and poor white children, regardless of their home background, achieve more. The Coleman report, it has been pointed out frequently, measures only the learning that takes place within fairly traditional classroom settings. It is entirely possible that radically different educational contexts or procedures will enable black or poor children to learn more readily in schools that are *not* integrated. But two qualifications must be considered: Within a broad range of standard educational practice, the Coleman report indicates that differences in educational facilities, such as pupil-teacher ratio or per-pupil expenditure, do not matter much. Secondly, reanalysis of the Coleman data and of the report *Racial Isolation in the Public Schools* shows that programs of compensatory education, programs that aim at improving the educational achievement of black children within segregated ghetto schools, have not worked despite heavy funding.

At best, we can remain hopeful, but realistically we must admit that what we know in any hard-headed way is that we are not certain how to improve the educational achievement of black or poor children where they go to school only with each other; we do know that we can improve their achievement by sending them to integrated schools, and we know as well that we can decrease racial bias in the process. We must remember, though, that integration implies increased centralization. It calls for an increase in those very characteristics of educational structure against which much contemporary reform has been directed, and justly so. One of the greatest weaknesses of education has been its bureaucratic form of organization; integration will only make that form more permanent. For advocates of both decentralization and integration, and I count myself among them, the future appears very bleak.

Educational radicals often fail to appreciate another dilemma, which the following incident illustrates. Seven poor mothers, disgusted with the treatment of their children in special classes for slow learners, began a little school of their own. Located in a vacant slum house, it had ten children taught by four undergraduates from a local university. When it came time to elect members for the city school board, the mothers decided that one of their number stand.

To plan the campaign they called on volunteers from the university and from a political party. At campaign meetings in the schoolhouse, the mothers sat on one side of the room, projecting anger at a school system that, they felt, ignored and insulted them and their children. On the other side sat the outsiders, dressed mostly in casual clothes, with longish hair, who saw in the mothers an indigenous community movement representing educational radicalism and participatory democracy. Pressed by the outsiders, the mothers offered personal stories of educational injustice, but very few specific educational objectives. When the candidate did adopt a platform, she advocated the reintroduction of report cards and corporal punishment; she opposed sex education.

The gulf that opened between the candidate and her imported supporters underlines the romantic fantasy at the core of much educational radicalism. For it expects a humanitarian and libertarian revolution in education to accompany a shift in power from the bureaucracy to the people. There are two distinguishable major strands in contemporary educational radicalism. One concentrates on the compulsory and bureaucratic structure of education, which it seeks to alter through the creation of alternatives to public schooling or through the redistribution of educational power to local communities within cities. This is the strand we have been considering. Another focuses on the spirit-breaking quality of current administrative and pedagogical practices and stresses the liberation of both teacher and student. Just as advocates of the former care more for community involvement than for administrative efficiency, the latter put happiness and warm human relations above subjects, skills, and classroom order.

It would be wrong to separate the two too sharply. Most educational radicals whose work I have read espouse both positions; the difference is a matter of emphasis. In fact, there is a premise, which we have noticed before, that the liberation of pedagogy will follow the liberation of the educational structure. It is clear, however, as the anecdote presented above demonstrates, that the two goals, pedagogical and political-structural, do not coexist in the minds of the constituency to which educational radicals appeal.

Nevertheless, despite—or perhaps because of—its visionary streak, the educational radicalism of the last several years has provided a beautiful, moving, and right-hearted body of pedagogical literature. The most effective of the radicals to me are experienced, deeply committed teachers who sensitively distill the history of their involvement with schools: I think of Sylvia Ashton-Warner, George Dennison, and A. S. Neill as examples. They are romantic about human potentiality and about education, and they are vulnerable as well to the logic-chopping ax of the academic critic. But that is irrelevant, for they are great teachers. And it is their presence, which manages to survive print, rather than any specific suggestion of method, that gives their writing its lucidity and inspiration. Educational radicalism gains its strength as well from the conditions it describes. Its proposals can be debated, but its critique is generally hard to fault; the school conditions that radicals attack are already appalling, as the film *High School* shows even more vividly than Jonathan Kozol's description of human destruction in the Boston schools.

The problem that educational radicalism as a critique now faces is how to maintain its urgency and driving force, for it is becoming popular, and its leading tenets, sometimes in distorted form, are expressed by a wide variety of people. At the mercy of lesser people, educational radicalism, like progressivism in an earlier era, rigidifies into a new orthodoxy that is nearly as dry and gutless as the old. Its history, I fear, will fall into the pattern cut earlier in the century by progressive educational thought, which, as a moment in intellectual history, combined an emphasis on community with a desire to liberate the child. In practice, though, as I have noted earlier, progressivism often added only a set of new wrinkles to an already overdeveloped educational bureaucracy. Rather than liberate the child from scholasticism, repression, and drill, the discovery of individual differences, as an instance, fueled the development of massive psychological testing and the creation of the guidance bureaucracy stretching from school counselors to university departments. Similarly, the professor of educational administration remains a more permanent artifact of the progressive era than Dewey's laboratory school. It was administrative values—the addition of supervisory positions, the war on inefficiency, the introduction of ability grouping—rather than the promotion of social reform through the democratic liberation of human intelligence, that most often defined the progressive spirit in practice.

Contemporary radicalism, in fact, may already be recapitulating the progressive experience. Here the Province of Ontario provides an especially clear example, with relevance for Americans as well as Canadians.

Not long ago, a provincial commission on the aims and objectives of education published a multicolored, illustrated, and self-consciously progressive report entitled *Living and Learning* (known locally as the Hall-Dennis report). It is a remarkable document and a shiny testament to the impact of educational radicalism. In it the representatives of the provincial Establishment, from whom the membership of the committee was drawn, declare themselves unequivocally in favor of child-centered schools for all; the reorganization of the curriculum into thematic, interdisciplinary components; and the virtual abandonment of age-grading throughout the school system. It is an official document simply unthinkable prior to the late 1960's.

Yet *Living and Learning*, despite its genuine obeisance to contemporary educational thought, remains a tame and essentially safe document (fit product of a Tory government), which never questions basic premises. It not only accepts compulsory education but intimates that its extension may become desirable; it fails to explore the existence of alternatives to public education; and, tellingly, it unquestioningly accepts traditional class-linked notions. One such notion, to which we should be alert by now, is the concept of cultural deprivation, a fancy way of labeling the lower orders inferior or, as I have observed above, depraved, in nineteenth-century terms. Another is the emphasis on the development of desirable (whose definition is no more specified now than in the time of Horace Mann) attitudes, which historically, of course, has meant the reformation of working-class morals according to the image in an idealized middle-class mirror. For all its progressive finish, alas, *Living and Learning* ducks the questions that matter most. At best it is castrated educational radicalism.

Living and Learning, I suspect, is the harbinger of a new progressivism that aspires to the radical mantle. That the movement will not deserve that distinction is hardly surprising. From the most cynical point of view, it is an old and usually brilliant trick of school people, like any bureaucrats, to dilute the strength of an attack by appearing to adopt the language of the enemy. Beyond that, however, there are weaknesses within educational radicalism itself, which have not been fully explored, and these bring us back to the story with which I began this section.

Educational radicalism has been offered as a cure for the pathology afflicting the education of the urban poor. But the mother from the slums whom I mentioned earlier may be more representative of the attitudes of poor people, than, say, Paul Goodman is. In fact, I suspect that what the poor want for their children is affluence, status, and a house in the suburbs rather than community, a guitar, and soul. They may prefer schools that teach their children to read and write and cipher rather than to feel and to be. If this is the case, then an uncomfortable piece of reality must be confronted: Educational radicalism is itself a species of class activity. It reflects an attempt at cultural imposition fully as much as the traditional educational emphasis on competition, restraint, and orderliness, whose bourgeois bias radicals are quick to excoriate.

There is a pathetic lack of fit between the poor and the schools, but educational radicalism offers us as much an ideology as a solution. Since the early nineteenth century, nostalgic intellectuals (like the democratic localists discussed earlier), frustrated by the scale and impersonality of urban life, have flirted recurrently with a vision of democratic, communally controlled, humanistic education. But factionalism, bigotry, and narrowness marked nineteenth-century rural towns at least as often as democratic communalism. If the racism in Cairo, Illinois, the persecution of teachers who discussed the United Nations in southern California, and the advocacy of report cards and corporal punishment by the indigenous candidate from the slums are at all representative, they suggest that people have changed very little, and that in turn should give pause to contemporary radicals.

All this is not meant to suggest that the radical critique of education is unfounded. It is profoundly true. Frighteningly often, schools destroy education and, more important, children. Unfortunately, a broadly acceptable alternative remains to be found. I doubt that we shall see an alternative soon, for educational radicalism already has become a new orthodoxy. Proof of that is *Radical School Reform*, a recent anthology of writings by contemporary radicals edited by Ronald and Beatrice Gross. It is a good anthology, for it represents the movement fairly, and it has thematic unity. But that is the point: The orthodoxy inheres in the success with which the movement can be anthologized and in the predictability of the Grosses' table of contents. The names there, ones we have heard again and again, are in fact those of the priests of the movement. In the last analysis, the anthology signals that educational radicalism has passed from a sect to a church. In the process it has lost its sting.

Four Suggestions for Reformers

This book has been an essay in historical social criticism; its tone has been largely negative. For that I think no apology is needed. Despite all that has been written on the ills of urban education, little has been said that helps to put those problems into a proper perspective by showing the development of the patterns and the establishment of the processes that have formed city school systems. The main difficulty with the traditional pietistic version of educational history is that it simply does not account for the schools that we now have. It is like the pietistic, conflict-free version of American history that would leave us today, were it true, amid a prospering, progressive, and consensual society marked by a happy, tolerant pluralism and equality for all men. We all know the real truth about society, and about schools as well. The purpose of this book has been to connect the history of the latter with that reality.

However, all this said, there are four positive suggestions for reformers that emerge from this analysis. The first relates to the purposes of education. It must be emphasized that, opinion to the contrary notwithstanding, people ask no more of schools today than they did a hundred and twenty-five years ago. Even then the schools were asked to do the impossible. As we have seen, the purpose of the school people has been more the development of attitudes than of intellect, and this continues to be the case. It is true, and this point must be stressed, of radical reformers as well as of advocates of law and order. The latter want the schools to stop crime and check immorality by teaching obedience to authority, respect for the law, and conformity to conventional standards. The former want the schools to reform society by creating a new sense of community through turning out warm, loving, noncompetitive people.

The human qualities that radical reformers seek in and through the schools are very beautiful ones; if achieved, they would give us a worthier and lovelier society. But it is no more realistic to charge the schools with the creation of such qualities than it is to expect them to fulfill traditional moralistic aims. Whatever values one attaches to the counterculture, whatever interpretation one gives to social conflict and crime, it is clear that the powers of schooling have been vastly overrated. Despite substantial financing and a captive audience, the schools have not been able to attain the goals set for them, with remarkably little change, for the last century and a quarter. They have been unable to do so because those goals have been impossible to fulfill. They require fundamental social reform, not the sort of tinkering that educational change has represented. If, by some miracle, the radical reformers were to capture the schools, and only the schools, for the next century, they would have no more success than educational reformers of the past.

The moral should be clear. Educational reformers should begin to distinguish between what formal schooling can and cannot do. They must separate the teaching of skills from the teaching of attitudes, and concentrate on the former. In actual fact, it is of course impossible to separate the two; attitudes adhere in any form of practice. But there is a vast difference between leaving the formation of attitudes untended and making them the object of education.

This is a radical position, despite the ordinary presumption to the contrary. In the popular version, schools once upon a time concentrated on the three R's. With no nonsense and remarkable success, they taught children to read, write, cipher, and spell. Then along came progressivism, which turned the schools into a combination social-service and life-adjustment bureau, forgetting, in the process, all about training in skills and the importance of the intellect. That history is simply false. The denigration of intellect and the neglect of skills have been continuing features of the history of public education; early school promoters believed quite as much as progressives that they were creating institutions to alleviate and prevent social problems.

There is a lot of talk about the foisting of middle-class values onto working-class children through the schools. In fact that happens to be an oversimplification, as Paul Goodman has pointed out beautifully in *Compulsory Mis-educa-*

tion. The values taught by the schools are not the tough, ascetic historic values of the bourgeois. Be that as it may, although schools do confront children with values that may be different from their own or from those of their parents, attempting to reverse the case may not prove desirable either, for the values of the poor may be those of the woman from the slum that I described earlier. The way out of this problem, it seems to me, is once again to take the schools out of the business of making attitudes. Have them attend to skills, especially, in the beginning, reading, and the question of whose values control the schools becomes largely irrelevant. For it is my premise that the desire that children become functionally literate and able to understand mathematics is nearly universal; it is as true of poor as of affluent parents.

To talk of cultural deprivation is to patronize the poor; it also is to deflect effort away from the education that they need. Poor children need to learn to read, not to visit museums, and I have seen no evidence of a correlation between the two. People have a right to hold whatever beliefs and whatever attitudes they please; that is the only consistent position for a civil libertarian. It follows that the attempt in schools to define one set of attitudes as superior to another, the attempt to teach patriotism, conventional morality, or even its opposite in a *compulsory* public institution represents a gross violation of civil rights.

My point is that educational theory should define strictly educational tasks and that schools should concentrate on those. Any such definition must include, at one end of the spectrum, fundamental skills; at the other, it must exclude the conscious attempt to formulate social attitudes. I am not arguing for what has been traditional in much educational practice; mental gymnastics for their own sake or the forced study of useless disciplines is indefensible. So is the rigid, authoritarian atmosphere of most schools. Schools should be made open, humane places for the simple reason that children have every right to be happy and to be treated with dignity and respect.

The atmosphere of the school relates to my second thought for reformers. The reformulation of educational purposes cannot be accomplished within current educational structures. Bureaucracy, as I hope I have made clear, is more than a form of organization; it is the crystallization of particular values. Through their structures, schools communicate a purpose; for contemporary schools, Robert Dreeben, in *On What Is Learned in Schools*, has made that very clear. School structure communicates particular norms; the learning of those norms has priority to the learning of skills. Those norms that are crystallized into contemporary educational forms reflect the purposes of education that have dominated American schools. Any radical reformulation of educational objectives, it follows, requires a radical restructuring of educational forms.

It is difficult to see the functional relationships between large size, economies of scale, bureaucratic organization, and so on, on the one hand, and learning to read, write, and do math, on the other. Unless the effectiveness of electronic computers proves revolutionary at these tasks (which I doubt), it is hard to see why the business of learning these things cannot be managed more simply, directly, and informally by skilled teachers working with small groups of children wherever they can find some space. The public can provide the equipment and materials and pay the salaries and rent, as now, but the activities do not have to be carried on within what we now call a school. The setting can be warm, colorful, comfortable, and humane without being expensive. Perhaps in some instances children need special facilities and special teachers, as in art, music, or history; perhaps even at an early age they should have access to laboratories for science. These facilities should be very good indeed. Children could go to them as they need and want to. It is not my intention to offer a detailed plan here. Rather, I just wish to emphasize what seems to me a very commonsensical position. Let us examine each of the activities children will undertake as they grow up and ask how it might best be handled, best in the sense of economy, of humaneness, of making the setting a happy one. In the process, we should avoid large institutions, bureaucratic organization, and complexity whenever anything else will serve as well.

It would be well if this reformed set of educational arrangements could be voluntary; compulsion should be removed on principle, wherever possible. However, and this is my third suggestion, the abolition of compulsion should be accompanied by radical changes in educational structure; it may be dangerous for children if it happens alone. Consider for a moment the possibilities inherent in abolishing compulsory schooling without making any other major social or educational changes. Parents might pressure children to leave school early in order to go to work; employers would exploit juvenile labor. We offer at present little worthwhile work to a young person uninterested in formal schooling, and, what is of most importance of all, we do not offer alternative ways of becoming educated or easy access back into schooling. Given the present rigid, sequential, age-graded system, the young person who leaves school early and later wants to re-enter faces major problems. Abolishing compulsory education could work against the interests of all children, especially the poor, if it were not accompanied by provisions to enable them to find worthwhile work and to resume formal education with financial support whenever they want to do so. The connection between level of schooling and employment opportunity will have to be broken as well, as it should be. All these things should be done. As Paul Goodman has argued, we must permit alternative ways for people to grow and to live. That is the real purpose of abolishing compulsory education. Otherwise, we might simply serve the needs of industry in search of cheap labor or of taxpayers whose only interest is lowering educational cost.

The same caution about balance applies to decentralization. My fourth suggestion is the point I made earlier: Decentralization should include a shift of power to teachers and students, away from administrators, as well as to local communities. Many of the recommendations for community control represent merely the exchange of one arbitrary governing authority for another. It is certainly true that parents could hardly do a worse job of running ghetto schools than educational bureaucracies have done. When the median math score of twelfth-grade children is grade six, it is impossible to argue with any honesty that community control will hurt educational achievement. But that is not enough. For decentralization to bring about improvements, the teacher as well as the school must be liberated.

There is no one way, nor even a few ways, of rightly arranging for education. There are many ways, and anyone who argues otherwise is foolish. Most arrangements should have, perhaps, certain features, and I have suggested some of them. But, for the most part, the particular form education should take in any one place should be worked out by the people involved. Professional educationists can offer a great deal of assistance, but the days when they should offer blueprints have ended. Let us be thankful, for that system has brought us to where we are: Too many children do not learn well and are unhappy in school; teachers suffer and lack autonomy; parents are dissatisfied; and economists warn of impending massive unemployment. Not even a college degree assures one a job any more. Aside from the people who live off the education system, and I do not mean the teachers, it has served no one very well. We are all its victims, and no one has done very much constructive about that for the last century. I should like to think that the time has come.

A Note on Sources,
Personal and Otherwise

The sources of this book are people as well as historical documents. I have talked and argued with, shown drafts to, tried ideas on, and received insights from, more people than I could possibly list. But I would like to mention a few of them by name. David Tyack read and argued with me about the chapter on Boston before it was published in its longer form; as well, our conversations throughout the last few years about urban education and his own research into the late nineteenth and early twentieth centuries have been extremely helpful. Similarly, my conversations with Clarence Karier and his own revisionist ideas about Dewey came at precisely the time when I needed help in putting together progressive educational thought and municipal reform. In the last few years I have also benefited greatly from Charles Bidwell's criticisms of my work. As in my earlier work, Dan Calhoun played an important role in this book, perhaps more important than he realizes: first by pointing me toward Lynn Marshall's "The Strange Stillbirth of the Whig Party" (*American Historical*

Review, 72 January, 1967); later by asking exactly the right question about an early draft of an essay on alternative models. During the last several years Stephan Thernstrom, too, has offered enormous encouragement and intelligent criticism.

As much as anyone, my students have contributed to the development of my ideas over the past five years. For their good and critical conversation on matters related directly to this book, I would especially like to thank Barbara Brenzel, Susan Houston, Gordon McLennan, Alison Prentice, and Peter Ross. During the summer of 1970 the students in my course on contemporary controversy in urban education contributed to the last chapter of this book by their refusal to let me get away easily with my arguments. The contributions of my wife, Edda, are very special; without her I am sure this book would still be undone.

This book is addressed to the "general reader," a person I have yet to meet but in whose existence publishers (and who am I to doubt them?) fervently believe. Consequently, I have dispensed throughout with the apparatus of scholarship. I refer readers who would like citations to a number of my previous writings, which document most of the material in this book: "From Voluntarism to Bureaucracy in American Education," *Sociology of Education* (Summer, 1971), a slightly different version of Chapter One; "The Emergence of Bureaucracy in Urban Education: The Boston Case, 1850–1884," *History of Education Quarterly*, two parts (Summer, 1968; Fall, 1968), a much more detailed account of the events recounted in Chapter Two; "The New Departure in Quincy, 1875–1881: The Nature of Nineteenth-Century Educational Reform," *New England Quarterly* (March, 1967), a close examination of Quincy under Francis Parker. *The Irony of Early School Reform: Educational Innovation in Mid-Nineteenth-Century Massachusetts* (Cambridge: Harvard University Press, 1968, reprinted by Beacon Press, 1970) contains documentation on points made throughout this discussion. And, finally, *School*

Reform: Past and Present (Boston: Little, Brown, 1971) is a book of readings where many of the documents that have influenced me most may be found.

Two writers more than any others have influenced my interpretation of contemporary social and cultural concerns. They are Theodore Roszak, through his brilliant book *The Making of the Counter-Culture* (Garden City: Doubleday, 1969), and Paul Goodman, who remains for me the wisest, most humane, and most insightful of contemporary social critics.

This is not the place for a detailed bibliographic discussion of American educational history. But some especially important books should be mentioned for the reader who wishes to pursue further some of the matters discussed in these pages. There is no adequate history of American education, no text or general survey to which I can with confidence refer the reader. *The Educating of Americans: A Documentary History* (Boston: Houghton-Mifflin, 1969), edited by Daniel Calhoun, is by far the best book of its kind, an original, insightful, and fascinating collection. Likewise, David Tyack's book of readings, *Turning Points in American Educational History* (Waltham, Mass.: Blaisdell, 1967), contains a great many useful documents, imaginatively arranged. Clarence Karier's *Man, Society and Education: A History of American Educational Ideas* (Chicago: Scott, Foresman, 1967), is a very fine over-all discussion of educational thought. Provocative and useful, too, is Rush Welter, *Popular Education and Democratic Thought in America* (New York: Columbia University Press, 1962).

The seminal essay in the revival of interest in the history of education that began in the 1960's is Bernard Bailyn's *Education in the Forming of American Society* (Chapel Hill: University of North Carolina Press, 1960), a brief excursion in hypothetical history. Although the demographic analysis of English and of Colonial society is proving that much of what Bailyn suggested about the family cannot be sustained by the

facts, the essay nevertheless remains a *tour de force* that must
be read by anyone who is seriously interested in American
education. The most recent and comprehensive discussion of
Colonial education is Lawrence Cremin's *American Education: The Colonial Experience* (New York: Harper & Row,
1970), an impressive work of scholarship with an old-fash-
ioned (in the best sense of the term) approach; its bibliog-
raphy is the most complete available on the subject. There are
extremely useful documents on both the Colonial period and
the first half of the nineteenth century in Robert H. Bremner,
ed., *Children and Youth in America: A Documentary History*
(Cambridge: Harvard University Press, 1970).

There is not a great deal written about the first half of the
nineteenth century that can be recommended. Certainly,
James McLachlan's *American Boarding Schools: A History*
(New York: Scribner's, 1970), a splendid survey of the subject, must be included in any list. For the most part, however,
the reader will have to go to journal articles; among the most
useful are Jonathan Messerli, "Localism and State Control in
Horace Mann's Reform of the Common Schools," *American
Quarterly*, 17 (Spring, 1965); David Tyack, "The Kingdom of
God and the Common School," *Harvard Educational Review*, 36 (Fall, 1966); Timothy Smith, "Protestant Schooling
and American Nationality, 1800–1850," *The Journal of American History*, 53 (March, 1967); and Daniel Calhoun, "From
Noah Webster to Chauncey Wright: The Intellectual as Prog-
nostic," *Harvard Educational Review*, 36 (Fall, 1966). For
books that treat less specialized subjects but provide important interpretive frameworks I recommend Oscar and Mary
Handlin, *Commonwealth: A Study of the Role of Government in the American Economy, Massachusetts, 1774–1861*
(New York: New York University Press, 1947), and Marvin
Myers, *The Jacksonian Persuasion* (Stanford, Calif.: Stanford
University Press, 1957). The history of education paralleled
the history of prisons, mental hospitals, and reform schools;

reading about other sorts of institutions thus illuminates the
subject of schools. The reader who wants to learn about the
history of education would therefore do well to examine
Gerald Grob's excellent book *The State and the Mentally Ill*
(Chapel Hill: University of North Carolina Press, 1966), and
Walter D. Lewis, *From Newgate to Dannemora* (Ithaca,
N.Y.: Cornell University Press, 1965).

For the progressive period the secondary literature about
education is not copious. There is, first, Lawrence Cremin's
The Transformation of the School (New York: Random
House, 1961). Although I disagree with Cremin's interpretation of progressivism, I have great admiration for this book,
which is a graceful and learned intellectual history. Raymond
Callahan, *Education and the Cult of Efficiency* (Chicago:
University of Chicago Press, 1962), contains a great deal of
useful data, although I would quarrel with much of his interpretation. Edward Krug, *The Shaping of the American High
School* (New York: Harper & Row, 1964), is an indispensable
source of information on the development of the high school
curriculum. David Tyack's work on the centralization of
schools and Clarence Karier's on Dewey and on the testing
movement, most of which remains unpublished, are writings
that anyone interested in these subjects should watch for with
some anticipation.

There is little published material on what went on within
schools and within communities during the late nineteenth and
early twentieth centuries. The most complete and useful data
we have about the twentieth century are to be found in Helen
and Robert Merrill Lynd's *Middletown* (New York: Harcourt, Brace, 1929), and *Middletown in Transition* (New
York: Harcourt, Brace, 1937). Of the more general books on
this period in American history, the one that has impressed
and influenced me most is Robert Wiebe, *The Search for Order, 1877–1920* (New York: Hill & Wang, 1967).

Moving closer to the present, the problem one finds is an embarrassment of riches. Books on educational reform seem to come out almost daily; I have long stopped trying to keep up with them. Of those I have read I have found the following most useful: Paul Goodman's *Growing Up Absurd* (New York: Random House, 1956), *Compulsory Mis-education* (New York: Horizon, 1964), and *The New Reformation* (New York: Random House, 1970) stand out as works of social and educational criticism. The mood of disenchanted students is captured well in Tom Seligson and Marc Libarle, eds., *The High School Revolutionaries* (New York: Random House, 1970). Henry Resnik, in *Turning on the System* (New York: Pantheon Books, Random House, 1970), offers a lucid and insightful history of a very recent movement of educational reform, a history depressingly easy to predict on the basis of past experience. Maurice Berube and Marilyn Gittell, in *Confrontation at Ocean-Hill Brownsville* (New York: Praeger, 1969), have provided a clear (as much as that subject can be) and intelligent book of readings representing a wide variety of points of view. Similarly, Ronald and Beatrice Gross, in *Radical School Reform* (New York: Simon & Schuster, 1970), have compiled a very useful anthology of contemporary viewpoints.

The history of Negro education remains, appallingly, unwritten. Henry Bullock has written a sometimes questionable survey in *A History of Negro Education in the South from 1619 to the Present* (Cambridge: Harvard University Press, 1967; paperback New York: Praeger, 1970). Louis Harlan's *Separate and Unequal: Public School Campaigns and Racism in the Southern Seaboard States, 1901–1915* (Chapel Hill: University of North Carolina Press, 1958) remains a more incisive and very useful source on Southern developments after the Civil War. Herbert Gutman's forthcoming book on the Reconstruction period promises to put the whole subject in a new perspective. On the point of view of black intellectuals, August Meir, *Negro Thought in America, 1880–1915*

(Ann Arbor: University of Michigan Press, 1963), is quite helpful.

Educators of every period have left documents that reveal their thought and their activities. Most school districts have records that enable one to reconstruct quite precisely what happened there. From school reports, censuses, and other sources it is possible to cull surprisingly large amounts of information about school attendance, school finances, teachers, and related subjects. Except for the writings of the most famous of educators, these sources have scarcely been tapped. That accounts for the massive ignorance about what happened and why it still persists concerning educational history, as I have mentioned throughout these pages. For anyone seriously interested in making more decisive our knowledge about how American education came to be, or in just finding out for himself, the material is at hand.

Index